SEASON TO TASTE

SEASON TO TASTE

REWRITING KITCHEN SPACE
IN CONTEMPORARY
WOMEN'S FOOD MEMOIRS

CAROLINE J. SMITH

University Press of Mississippi / Jackson

The University Press of Mississippi is the scholarly publishing agency of the Mississippi Institutions of Higher Learning: Alcorn State University, Delta State University, Jackson State University, Mississippi State University, Mississippi University for Women, Mississippi Valley State University, University of Mississippi, and University of Southern Mississippi.

www.upress.state.ms.us

The University Press of Mississippi is a member of the Association of University Presses.

Any discriminatory or derogatory language or hate speech regarding race, ethnicity, religion, sex, gender, class, national origin, age, or disability that has been retained or appears in elided form is in no way an endorsement of the use of such language outside a scholarly context.

Copyright © 2023 by University Press of Mississippi
All rights reserved

First printing 2023
∞

Library of Congress Cataloging-in-Publication Data

Names: Smith, Caroline J., 1974– author.
Title: Season to taste : rewriting kitchen space in contemporary women's food memoirs / Caroline J. Smith.
Other titles: Ingrid G. Houck series in Food and Foodways.
Description: Jackson : University Press of Mississippi, 2023. | Series: Ingrid G. Houck series in food and foodways | Includes bibliographical references and index.
Identifiers: LCCN 2022051958 (print) | LCCN 2022051959 (ebook) | ISBN 9781496845610 (hardback) | ISBN 9781496845627 (trade paperback) | ISBN 9781496845634 (epub) | ISBN 9781496845641 (epub) | ISBN 9781496845658 (pdf) | ISBN 9781496845665 (pdf)
Subjects: LCSH: Women food writers. | Food writing—Social aspects. | Food writing—Political aspects. | Cookbooks—Social aspects. | Cookbooks—Political aspects. | Kitchens—Social aspects. | Kitchens—Design and construction. | Food—Social aspects.
Classification: LCC TX644 .S65 2023 (print) | LCC TX644 (ebook) | DDC 808.06/6641—dc23/eng/20230127
LC record available at https://lccn.loc.gov/2022051958
LC ebook record available at https://lccn.loc.gov/2022051959

British Library Cataloging-in-Publication Data available

To Henry Smith Stearns—the best I've cooked up yet.

CONTENTS

ACKNOWLEDGMENTS. ix

INTRODUCTION: Serve It Forth 3

1. DESIGN CHALLENGE: *Better Homes and Gardens*
and the Changing Space of the US American Kitchen 21

2. "A WOMAN'S MOST REWARDING WAY OF LIFE": The
Feminist/Housewife Debate and Contemporary
Women's Response 37

3. WINKING WHILE WE BAKE: Recoding Kitchen Space
in Contemporary Food Writing. 49

4. KITCHEN SPACES: Sites of Resistance and Transformation. 67

5. THE GENDER POLITICS OF MEAT: The Foodie Romance
and Julie Powell's *Cleaving*. 89

6. BLOG HER: Transgressing Narrative Boundaries. 105

viii Contents

AFTERWORD: Writer. Eater. Cook. 121

NOTES. 127

BIBLIOGRAPHY. 139

INDEX 157

ACKNOWLEDGMENTS

This project has been a long time in the making, and as a result, I have a list (that spans over a decade) of people to thank for their love and encouragement.

First of all, thank you to all of those individuals whom I have worked with at the University Press of Mississippi: Kelly Burch, Corley Longmire, Joey Brown, Todd Lape, Jackson Watson, Craig Gill, and especially Lisa McMurtray and Emily Snyder Bandy. I appreciate your interest in my project and the time and attention you gave to it. Many thanks to Holly Day for her work indexing this book. A special thank you to Lindsey Cleworth for her cover design. Chef's kiss.

This project would not have been possible without the financial support of The George Washington University. I'd also like to extend thanks to the librarians and staff at the Sallie Bingham Center for Women's History and Culture at Duke University.

Thank you to my wonderful current (and former) George Washington librarian friends, Ann Brown, Shira Eller, Bill Gillis, and Tina Plottel, for your research expertise. I also greatly appreciate the support of my fellow faculty members in the University Writing Program, particularly the members of the Anti-Racism Committee. Specifically, I'd like to thank Abby Wilkerson, Danika Myers, and Michael Svoboda for their extra encouragement when it was most needed. Finally, I am always incredibly appreciative of my George

Washington students who—in the classroom—read, researched, and wrote about many of the texts included in *Season to Taste*. To Audrey Scagnelli's fall 2010 section of UW1020, I am particularly grateful.

Personally, I am forever thankful for my supportive family of origin (the Smiths) and my extended family (the Stearns). Kathi Ketcheson, thank you for introducing me to Powell's Bookstore. And Parker Nielsen, thank you for always inquiring with interest about my project at every Thanksgiving, Christmas, and Easter dinner over the years. I also owe a great deal of gratitude to all the wonderful families in my Takoma Moms' Group and Purple School Cohort; specific individuals who deserve extra kudos are Sarah, Alyssa, Erik, Aga, Heidi, Bronwen (a terrific North Carolina host!), and Rachel (a kindred pop culture spirit). And to the other mothers in my life, Corinne, Roberta, and Kate, I cherish our friendships.

Finally, my little circle of love at home—both human and canine—Frank, Henry, Ruby, Halle, and Pippin, you make the kitchen a little warmer and the meals much more delicious.

SEASON TO TASTE

INTRODUCTION

SERVE IT FORTH

On 7 August 2009, the movie *Julie & Julia* opened to complimentary reviews and a positive public reception. The film, directed by Nora Ephron, was adapted from the equally successful 2005 memoir *Julie & Julia: 365 Days, 524 Recipes, 1 Tiny Apartment Kitchen* by Julie Powell. Three years earlier, on a whim, Powell, who was disgruntled with her job as a government employee, began cooking her way through Julia Child's 1961 *Mastering the Art of French Cooking*. With the encouragement of her husband, she began a blog titled *The Julie/Julia Project*, where she recorded her adventures. The popularity of the blog resulted in a subsequent book deal with Little, Brown & Company and then the film adaptation, which starred Amy Adams as Powell and Meryl Streep as Julia Child. Film critics such as A. O. Scott of the *New York Times* and food bloggers such as Alejandra Ramos (*Always Order Dessert*) responded favorably to the film, particularly to the Julia Child storyline, and the movie came in second place at the box office, grossing $20.1 million on opening weekend and being outdone only by *G.I. Joe* (Corliss).[1]

Ephron's film and its associated texts serve as tangible examples of US Americans' preoccupation with all things food during the first two decades of the twenty-first century. These texts also trouble several significant oppositional structures, or binaries, often upheld by US Americans—private/home/feminine and public/work/masculine. For example, with the publication of *Mastering the Art of French Cooking* (public), Julia Child taught postwar middle-class, white US American housewives how to cook French food in their home kitchens (private). Her popular television series, *The French Chef* (public), which ran from 1963 to 1973, featured Child's cooking demonstrations to this same demographic (private). Her later cooking series (public) garnered an equally substantial following (private). Some of the later television series, such as *In Julia's Kitchen with Master Chefs*, took place in her home kitchen (private), which was outfitted appropriately to serve as a television set (public).[2] Like Child, Powell cooked in her home kitchen (private), but her chronicling on her blog brought a public element to her personal act of cooking. Readers could follow Powell's cooking experiment on her blog, experiencing her successes and failures as they read.

Season to Taste: Rewriting Kitchen Space in Contemporary Women's Food Memoirs meditates on these private/public divides through the analysis of food writing by women published during the first two decades of the twenty-first century. This food writing has been a popular subset of the larger food movement, and it serves as an interesting site for examining the gender politics associated with both the preparation and consumption of food. Between 2000 and 2010, many contemporary US American women were returning to the private space of the kitchen, writing about their experiences in that space, and then publishing their memoirs for the larger public to consume. In *Season to Taste*, I examine selected food writing (specifically writing that includes recipes) published during this time period in order to consider the ways in which these women are rewriting this kitchen space and renegotiating their relationships with food. In turn, I examine how this reinterpretation affects their roles within the private sphere of the home as well as the public sphere of the world of publishing (whether print or digital publication). These texts, I argue, explode the divide of private/feminine and public/masculine in both content and form and trouble the genres of recipe writing, diary writing, and memoir. Ultimately, in *Season to Taste*, I consider the ways in which these women writers, through the act of preparing and consuming food, encourage readers to reconsider the changing gender politics of the kitchen.

In her introduction to *The Best American Food Writing* (2018), Ruth Reichl, the contemporary doyenne of the food world, begins: "Food writing is stepping out. . . . For far too long it's been the timid little sister . . . , afraid to raise its voice" (xv). A writer for both the *New York Times* and the *Los Angeles Times*, long-time editor for *Gourmet* magazine, and the author of several best-selling food books, Reichl has been around long enough to chronicle the US American public's complicated relationship with food writing. Reichl remembers "an era when America's interest in food was so minimal that serious writers refused to choose it as their subject. It was, they thought, beneath them" (xv). Silvia Killingsworth, the series editor, agrees: "Food writing itself has not always been taken seriously" (ix).[3] But more recently, both women acknowledge, food is a topic of writing for novelists, scientists, and sportswriters alike.[4] As Reichl writes, "Americans have changed their mind about food. We've shaken off our indifference, transformed our outlook, and recognized that food offers a unique perspective on almost every subject" (xvii).

As Reichl and Killingsworth observe, US Americans at the start of the twenty-first century became increasingly preoccupied with all things food; this interest swelled for a variety of reasons. In *The Best American Food Writing*, Reichl credits this trend in part to television programming and the rise of the celebrity chef.[5] On television, shows like the Food Network's *Iron Chef America* (2004–2018) and *The Next Food Network Star* (2005–present) abounded.[6] The success of this programming prompted other networks to follow suit, capitalizing on this trend; most notably is Bravo's series *Top Chef* (2006–present).[7] The success of these television programs provided these celebrity chefs with a platform for marketing both cookbooks and kitchenware lines.[8] Bravo has even created a Top Chef University, which launched in 2010; those interested in learning more about cooking can enroll in the school and be taught online by previous contestants.

Other cultural forces, of course, were at work, too. Food was featured on the big screen from documentaries such as Robert Kenner's *Food, Inc.* (2008) to feature films such as *Julie & Julia*.[9] In February 2010, America's first lady at the time, Michelle Obama, launched her Let's Move! campaign with its emphasis on healthy eating and exercise. April 2016 marked her eighth and final year of planting in the White House garden, an initiative that sparked a renewed interest in gardening and consuming organic foods (Zak).[10] And, in many major metropolitan areas, the food truck craze took over; in many US American cities food trucks lined the streets, selling everything from macaroni and cheese to *jamón ibérico* sandwiches to lobster rolls to red velvet cupcakes.[11]

Alongside this general interest in food, all kinds of writing about food surged between 2000 and 2010. The genre of food writing, as Lynn Z. Bloom explains in her 2008 article, "Consuming Prose: The Delectable Rhetoric of Food Writing," is vast. Writers of fiction and nonfiction, she notes, have often been "devoted to food" or included "significant food-related scenes" in their work (348). In her essay, she continues to detail the various genres that have preoccupied themselves with food, including novels, essays, autobiography, travel writing, and what she deems "more research-oriented works about food itself" (349).

While there were fiction texts produced during this decade (Andrea Israel and Nancy Garfinkel's 2009 *The Recipe Club: A Novel about Food and Friendship* and Erica Bauermeister's 2009 *The School of Essential Ingredients*, for example), it was nonfiction writing about food that really took a foothold in the publishing industry, and these nonfiction works took a variety of forms. Cookbooks, always a popular form of food writing, continued to thrive in the publishing industry in the opening decades of the twenty-first century.[12]

Cookbooks authors such as Julia Child, Rachael Ray, and Martha Stewart became recognizable names for many US Americans; specific cookbooks such as *The Best Recipes in the World* (2005) by Mark Bittman and *Think Like a Chef* (2000) by Tom Colicchio experienced financial success upon publication.[13] There were food essays published in food-centered publications, such as *Saveur*, as well as in more general interest publications, such as the *New Yorker*. Other food writers (e.g., Mark Kurlansky, *Salt: A World History of Food* and Jennifer Lee, *The Fortune Cookie Chronicles: Adventures in the World of Chinese Food*) provided a historical perspective on food trends. Another subset of food writing included food manifestos, which ranged from Barbara Kingsolver's *Animal, Vegetable, Miracle* (2007), which advocated for US Americans to change their eating habits, to Michael Pollan's *In Defense of Food: An Eater's Manifesto* (2008), which encouraged US Americans to adopt healthier food choices.

Much of this food writing is autobiographical in nature. Food is often used in these texts as a device to structure the narrative, whether providing a central focus for the autobiography or serving as a theme for individual chapters. For instance, food critics such as Reichl (*Tender at the Bone*, 1998; *Comfort Me with Apples: More Adventures at the Table*, 2001; and *Garlic and Sapphires*, 2005) chronicle their culinary adventures in longer, narrative form, while other writers, such as Eduardo Machado and Michael Domitrovich in *Tastes Like Cuba: An Exile's Hunger for Home* (2007) and Kate Moses in *Cakewalk* (2010), recount childhood memories through the meals that were eaten. Still others, such as Anthony Bourdain's *Kitchen Confidential: Adventures in the Culinary Underbelly* (2000) and Dalia Jurgensen's *Spiced: A Pastry Chef's True Stories of Trial by Fire, After-Hours Exploits, and What Really Goes on in the Kitchen* (2009), take readers behind the scenes of the restaurant industry.

Another popular and ever-growing subset of food writing during this time was food blogging, which often combined stories with recipes.[14] While it is hard to get an accurate gauge as to how many food blogs existed between 2000 and 2010, in *Food*

Blogs, Postfeminism, and the Communication of Expertise: Digital Domestics (2020), Alane L. Presswood estimates the total number of active food bloggers at the time of the publication of her book to be upward of 20,000 (1). The most successful of these bloggers, such as Deb Perelman of *Smitten Kitchen* and Shauna James Ahern of *Gluten-Free Girl*, often received book deals.

While both men and women writers explore their relationships with the food that they eat and make sense of those experiences by integrating complementary recipes within their narratives, women, in particular, were a strong presence in the field of autobiographical food writing. As of December 2021, on the site Goodreads ("the largest site for readers and book recommendations in the world"), the link devoted to "Popular Food Writing Books" lists 3,269 books in this genre ("About Goodreads"). Of the first ten entries listed, six of those books are written by women, and four of those books are written by men ("Shelves>Food Writing>Popular Food Writing Books").[15] *Newsweek* writer Jennie Yabroff picked up on this trend, noting in her 2010 article "Touchy-Feely Food Memoirs," "It seems every month brings a new crop of food memoirs, the majority of them by women." Her article mentions Moses's *Cakewalk* and Kim Severson's *Spoon Fed* (2010) as well as three of Reichl's memoirs; all five of these books were written sometime between 1998 and 2010. Additionally, skimming lists such as "Popular Food Memoir Books" on Goodreads reveals that food memoirs such as Madhur Jaffrey's *Climbing the Mango Trees: A Memoir of a Childhood in India* (2006), Kathleen Flinn's *The Sharper Your Knife, the Less You Cry: Love, Laughter, and Tears at the World's Most Famous Cooking School* (2007), and Fuchsia Dunlop's *Shark's Fin and Sichuan Pepper: A Sweet-Sour Memoir of Eating in China* (2008) were all published after 2005 and in consecutive years. Other food memoirs, such as Julie Powell's 2005 *Julie & Julia* and Gabrielle Hamilton's *Blood, Bones, Butter: The Inadvertent Education of a Reluctant Chef* (2011), created quite a buzz upon their releases.[16] And, as mentioned previously, food blogs, whose narrative approaches were similar to the print memoirs mentioned, attracted and maintained a host of devoted readers during this time period.[17]

These women food writers, producing autobiographical food writing in the first decade of the twenty-first century, are not the first women writers to explore their relationship with the kitchen and with food. Writers such as M. F. K. Fisher (1908–1992), Laurie Colwin (1944–1992), and Judith Jones (1924–2017) experienced success in their time. However, unlike the works examined here, their writing was not necessarily part of a larger cultural trend in publishing in their given historical moments; instead, they were singular voices. By contrast, the women food writers looked at in *Season to Taste: Rewriting Kitchen Space in Contemporary Women's Food Memoirs* have been part of a larger movement—both in US American culture in general and in the publishing industry specifically.

While US Americans' interest in watching, reading, and writing stories about food has swelled of late, academia has been slower to embrace the study. In *Food: The Key Concepts* (2008), Warren Belasco attributes this hesitancy to three things: (1) the "dualism that prizes mind over body," (2) the concept of separate spheres (the public sphere, coded male, being valued over the private, coded female, sphere), and (3) "technological utopianism," which encouraged US Americans to abandon the work of the kitchen in favor of labor-saving devices. Nevertheless, scholars in cultural anthropology, as Carole Counihan and Penny Van Esterik explain in *Food and Culture: A Reader* (1997), as well as those in the discipline of folklore were among the first to seriously consider food as a topic of study. As Lucy M. Long notes in her introduction to *The Food and Folklore Reader* (2015):

> Food has been included within folklore studies since the late 1800s. The focus originally was on "folk foods," those that were traditional to groups historically tied to the land, and on "folklore about food," beliefs and customs surrounding food. . . . [B]eginning in the 1960s and 1970s, folklorists explored "food as folklore," a domain of

> cultural and social activity in which groups and individuals interactively and creatively construct, maintain, and negotiate meaningful connections to their pasts, places, and other people. (1)

At the start of the twentieth century, other disciplines began more actively interrogating the role of food in US American culture. The discipline of food studies, generally defined by Jeff Miller and Jonathan Deutsch in *Food Studies: An Introduction to Research Methods* (2009) as "[t]he study of the relationships between food and the human experience" (3), garnered more attention. Counihan and Van Esterik begin the introduction to the third edition of *Food and Culture: A Reader* (2013) with this: "In 1997, when we proposed the first *Food and Culture Reader*, we had to persuade Routledge of the important of publishing it. In 2012, Routledge had to persuade us to produce a third edition" (1). The anthology includes sections with titles such as "Hegemony and Difference: Race, Class, and Gender" and "Challenging, Contesting, and Transforming the Food System" with essays by well-known authors such as Margaret Mead, Roland Barthes, Sidney Mintz, Susan Bordo, and Eric Schlosser. Other topics, such as food safety, food insecurity, and the ethics of eating, are all areas of inquiry in this growing, interdisciplinary, scholarly movement.

Subsets of feminist scholarship, which is interdisciplinary in nature, has focused on intersections between gender and food culture. Arlene Avakian's 2005 work *Through the Kitchen Window: Women Explore the Intimate Meaning of Food and Cooking* (1997) was particularly significant and included essays by such influential writers as Dorothy Allison, Maya Angelou, and Marge Piercy. This collection called for a reconsideration of the role that the kitchen has played in women's lives, and the essays included often questioned the assumption that insignificant "work" occurred in the private sphere of the kitchen. In the spirit of Alice Walker's essay "In Search of Our Mothers' Gardens" (1983), the writers included in Avakian's work asked readers to reconsider "women's work" (i.e., cooking) as its own form of art. Avakian's subsequent work, an anthology coedited with Barbara Haber titled *From Betty Crocker to Feminist Food Studies: Critical Perspective on Women and Food* (2005), took a critical, feminist examination of food culture. The essays included in this work are grouped under the headings "The Marketplace," "Histories," "Representations," and "Resistances"; topics vary from examining the evolution of baby food ("Feeding Baby, Teaching Mother: Gerber and the Evolution of Infant Food and Feeding Practices in the United States") to a reading of Fannie Flagg's *Fried Green Tomatoes at the Whistle Stop Café* (1987). Sherrie Inness, a feminist, literary, cultural critic, authored two books (*Dinner Roles: American Women and Culinary Culture*, 2001, and *Secret Ingredients: Race, Class, and Gender at the Dinner Table*, 2006) and edited a number of anthologies that focus on identity politics and food. Both Inness and the authors included in her anthologies take interdisciplinary approaches to analyzing the subject matter by applying both feminist and cultural studies methodology to the work that they examine.[18]

While there has been excellent work done on feminism and food generally, there has been very little analysis of women's food writing with recipes, specifically. Literature scholars have taken time to analyze food moments in varied genres (e.g., poetry, drama, fiction) written by writers such as Emily Dickinson, Virginia Woolf, and Kate Chopin.[19] Feminist literary scholars have produced work that critically examines the genre of women's autobiography, and there has also been some significant scholarship on cookbooks.[20] However, women's food memoirs with recipes, specifically, have not found a firm foothold in a particular discipline. Traci Marie Kelly (2001), Alison D. Goeller (2005), and Jessica Lyn Van Slooten (2008) have examined the genre. Likewise, the more recent work of Arlene Avakian (2014), Kimberly D. Nettles-Barcelón (2017), and Lynn Z. Bloom (2017) address women's food memoirs with recipes exclusively. Vivian Nun Halloran's *The Immigrant Kitchen* (2016) is one of the few monographs that examines women's food memoirs with recipes in depth. In her work, Nun Halloran focuses on the work of both male and female writers, such as Eduardo Machado and Madhur Jaffrey, looking at how these writers use food to better understand their immigrant identities.

Season to Taste: Rewriting Kitchen Space in Contemporary Women's Food Memoirs intends to pick up where Nun Halloran's and Van Slooten's work leaves off. Nun Halloran provides the first in-depth analysis of food memoirs with recipes; however, she does not focus exclusively on women. Van Slooten's analysis, which examines both Hesser's and Powell's texts, looks at the way in which the two texts "represent a new hybrid genre" by combining journalistic writing, romance, and food writing.[21] Toward the end of her essay, Van Slooten identifies what I see as a strong trend in contemporary women's food writing in general—the reimaging of the space of the kitchen from a place of oppression to one of liberation.

Season to Taste continues, then, the work that Van Slooten has done, examining the genre of food writing with recipes. Over the course of this study, I consider how women writers reflect on their relationships with their kitchens. What, if any, are the gendered expectations associated with that kitchen space in the early twenty-first century? How do these writers interrogate many of the binary oppositions associated with the space of the kitchen and kitchen culture? How do women in these texts both prepare and consume food as related to their identities? And finally, in what ways are these writers exploding the public/masculine and private/feminine divide in both content and form? I chose to work exclusively with women's food writing that includes recipes because, as Nun Halloran observes, food writing with recipes is "a complex and engaging mass media product simultaneously catering to multiple reading constituencies and doing different types of cultural work" (5). Examining the autobiographical accounts of these authors and their accompanying recipes individually presents rich opportunities for analysis; the analysis becomes even more layered when they are examined in conversation with one another. The contemporary women authors examined here write kitchen spaces that become in Van Slooten's words "a place of true transformation" (401). While previous generations of US American women may have seen the kitchen as a powerful symbol of women's oppression, the contemporary women writers examined here feel drawn to that space, despite the previous negative connotations for occupying it, and in their texts, they puzzle out what this space means for them in the twenty-first century.

Season to Taste begins with a historical and visual analysis of the space of the kitchen, as represented by *Better Homes and Gardens*, and from there I analyze the discourse of the second wave feminist movement (the feminist movement of the 1960s), particularly in regard to the public versus private sphere. It is important to note that both *Better Homes and Gardens* and the rhetoric of the second wave feminist movement put middle- to upper-class, heterosexual, white US American women at their centers. While *Better Homes and Gardens* does not explicitly define its audience as white, the publication's primary readership is middle- to upper-class, white US American women.[22] Likewise, the second wave feminist movement that arose in the early 1960s to address women's inequality at home and in the workplace privileged the concerns of white women. The movement's leaders, such as Betty Friedan and Gloria Steinem, and other influential voices of the movement, such as Kate Millet and Carol Hanisch, largely consisted of white women, and in years since, the movement has been significantly criticized for the way in which it minimized and sometimes ignored the concerns of working-class women, women of color, and the LGBTQ+ community.

Consequently, popular cultural representations of the kitchen and cooking as well as the image of the housewife tend to privilege the images and experiences of white women. This historical context is important to keep in mind when reading the first two chapters of *Season to Taste*. In chapter 1, "Design Challenge: *Better Homes and Gardens* and the Changing Space of the US American Kitchen," I examine the physical space of the kitchen, interrogating the ways in which its redesign over the past decades has mirrored middle- to upper-class, white US American women's changing roles. Here, I look at editions of *Better Homes and Gardens* from 1960 to 2010 for the way in which the magazine imagined the space of the kitchen for its readers. While the kitchen features prominently in contemporary editions of the magazine, the kitchen has not always played such a predominant role. In fact, in the 1960s, the magazine placed much more importance on the living spaces of the home, particularly the den or the family room—a stark difference from the kitchen's hyperpresence in contemporary issues of the magazine. This shift in representation raises interesting questions about the historical role of the kitchen in the US American home. As its readers' roles evolved, the private space of the kitchen became a more publicly enjoyed space, shifting to a more central location in the home and being occupied by family members other than the female head of the household.

In chapter 2, "'A Woman's Most Rewarding Way of Life': The Feminist/Housewife Debate and Contemporary Women's Response," I look at the way in which discourse associated with the second wave feminist movement of the early 1960s polarized the roles of feminist and housewife and encouraged middle- to upper-class, white US American women to exchange the private sphere of the home for the public sphere of the workforce. These binaries (housewife/feminist and private/public) influenced the way in which women regarded their relationships to their kitchen space and their preparation and consumption of food. I begin my analysis of contemporary women's food writing in this chapter, examining the early food writing of Ruth Reichl. The focus of this chapter, Reichl's memoir *Comfort Me with Apples: More Adventures at the Table* (2001), was published during the early twenty-first century, but in it, Reichl details her experiences in the late 1970s as she rises to food-writing fame from her position as a restaurant critic at *New West* magazine to her work for the *Los Angeles Times* as a restaurant critic and food editor. In the spirit of second wave feminist discourse, Reichl strives to clearly establish herself as a professional. She aligns her text with the literary tradition of the memoir rather than that of the cookbook.

I begin chapter 3, "Winking While We Bake: Recoding Kitchen Space in Contemporary Food Writing," with a broad analysis of the rhetorical strategies of third wave feminist publications such as *Bitch* and *BUST*.[23] Unlike the rhetoric of the second wave feminist movement, the third wave feminist movement (the feminist movement of the 1990s) does not characterize the home as a place of imprisonment; rather, contemporary feminist discourse of this time period "recodes" the space of the home as a place that women can occupy while creating, enjoying, and even profiting from the work produced there.[24] Central to this chapter is my examination of the way in which racial politics plays a role in this return to the kitchen. While the rhetoric of third wave feminism has been quick to acknowledge the shortcomings of the previous feminist movements in regard to lack of inclusivity and while the leaders of the third wave feminist movement have included prominent women of color such as Rebecca Walker, daughter of writer and activist Alice Walker, the movement is often still criticized for its focus on the issues and concerns of its white audience. The question then becomes, "Who, according to the rhetoric of the third wave feminist movement, are these women who are returning to the kitchen and recoding this space?" As Kimberly D. Nettles-Barcelón offers in "Women and Entrepreneurial Food-Work: Second Acts, 'New Domesticity,' and the Continuing Significance of Racialized Difference," much of the recent discourse surrounding women's return to the kitchen focuses on one type of woman, leaving out a vast amount of the US American population, including "women of color, working class women, queer women, 'older women,' and unmarried women" (224–25).

This chapter foregrounds the work of food blogger Jocelyn Delk Adams (*Grandbaby Cakes*), who demonstrates this shift in representing the home kitchen and cook. As a Black woman, Delk Adams adopts the persona of Friedan's "happy housewife heroine." Her performance of the stereotypical 1950s housewife recodes that image for viewers. In doing so, she also invokes past depictions of Black women in the kitchen, calling into question the stereotypical representations that we see of Black women in this space. Her blog and her cookbook (*Grandbaby Cakes: Modern Recipes, Vintage Charm, Soulful Memories*, 2015) lift up the food work of past generations of Black women in order to remedy the incomplete and often false narrative that US American viewers and readers often receive about Black women in the space of the kitchen.

In chapter 4, "Kitchen Spaces: Sites of Resistance and Transformation," I examine two texts—Giulia Melucci's *I Loved, I Lost, I Made Spaghetti* (2010) and Kim Sunée's *Trail of Crumbs: Hunger, Love, and the Search for Home* (2009)—for the way in which they challenge assumptions about women's relationships with the food that they prepare and eat as well as the relationships that these women have with their bodies. Both Melucci's and Sunée's books were published as the popular fiction phenomenon known as chick lit was waning, and like those books, Melucci and Sunée chronicle their times as young women living in metropolitan areas and navigating their love relationships. Unlike chick lit, which often presents heroines struggling with their body weight and other consumption practices (such as shopping and sex), *I Loved, I Lost, I Made Spaghetti* and *Trail of Crumbs* resist the standard, often negative, messaging that women receive about their relationships with food. US American popular culture often encourages women to serve as the nurturers of others, eschewing the food that they prepare. This messaging reinforces the idea that women need to suppress their own appetites and be fastidious managers of their consumption. Sunée's and Melucci's memoirs, I argue, serve as a site of resistance; the preparation of food and the enjoyment of it are a vital component to these women writers' growth and development. Additionally, as an Asian American woman, Sunée must push back against expectations that her white friends and family have for her.[25] She does so by cooking and eating food that resists classification, preparing dishes that draw on various ethnic identities. In doing so, she also constructs a self-image that contests the prescribed idealization of (white) womanhood that various popular culture mediums often present to its consumers.

Chapter 5, "The Gender Politics of Meat: The Foodie Romance and Julie Powell's *Cleaving*," focuses on Julie Powell's second memoir, *Cleaving: A Story of Marriage, Meat, and Obsession* (2009). While Powell is best known for her blog and subsequent book *Julie & Julia*, *Cleaving* has been given less attention even though it is, arguably, the more interesting of the two. The book chronicles Powell's extramarital affair, her separation from her husband, and her attempts to heal herself through an apprenticeship to a family-owned butcher in the Catskills. In this chapter, I examine how in *Cleaving* Powell attempts to deconstruct not only her earlier memoir but also what literary critic Jessica Lyn Van Slooten has labeled the genre of the "foodie romance." This genre, Van Slooten argues, "capitalize[s] on the . . . romance, chick lit, and foodie memoir trends" and "chronicle[s] the pleasures and complications of relationships and consumption." Many of these texts (for example, Amanda Hesser's *Cooking for Mr. Latte*, 2003 and Elizabeth Bard's *Lunch in Paris: A Love Story, with Recipes*, 2010) adopt classic romance tropes, and they often position women and men in traditional gender roles when it comes to the space of the kitchen. *Cleaving* responds to these texts by detailing the dissolution of a marriage (not the fairytale romance) simultaneously with Powell's learning the very grisly art of butchering. Powell adopts the tools of the butcher and carves out a narrative in opposition to the foodie romances that have come before it.

My final chapter, "Blog Her: Transgressing Narrative Boundaries," examines the genre of food blogging, looking specifically at the work of Molly Wizenberg (author of the blog *Orangette*) and Shauna James Ahern (author of the blog *Gluten-Free Girl*).[26] Unlike most of the published food writing analyzed previously, these food memoirs are self-published; these bloggers post stories and recipes on a daily or weekly basis to their own blog sites. On one hand, their work resembles the more traditional genres of the diary and cookbook.

Yet, their blogs also contain features that are not representative of those respective genres. These blogs, then, become a hybrid form of food writing—one that draws upon both the private tradition of diary writing and the public traditions of the food memoir and the cookbook. By structurally transgressing narrative conventions, Wizenberg and Ahern contribute a new chapter to the history of women and food writing.

I conclude my examination of women food writers in my afterword, "Writer. Eater. Cook.," where I return to the work of Ruth Reichl. As I demonstrated in chapter 2, Reichl was careful in her memoirs to position herself as a professional restaurant critic, distancing herself from the home kitchen. In recent years, however, Reichl's work has responded to American women's changing relationships with the kitchen. Reichl's later work, such as her novel *Delicious!* (2014) and *My Kitchen Year: 136 Recipes That Saved My Life* (2015), responds to these shifts in cultural consciousness, revealing and resolving for herself some of the historical tensions between home/work, private/public, housewife/feminist.

In *Food: The Key Concepts* (2008), Warren Belasco reflects upon the complications that academics can face in studying women and food. He writes, "While more women began to enter all fields of academia in the 1960s, it took several decades before scholars could begin to consider the traditional female ghetto of domesticity without Victorian-era blinders and prejudices, and even today, feminists who do treasure their cooking heritage and skills may risk the hostility of colleagues who feel that women should move on to more 'serious' pursuits" (3). While he acknowledges that there has been "significant and largely sympathetic reappraisals of women's food work," he also notes that "the identification of food with oppression still slants the scholarship—as evidenced, perhaps, by the fact that there may be more research devoted to women's eating disorders than to women's positive connections to food" (3).[27] In each chapter of *Season to Taste*, I provide readers with examinations of the ways in which contemporary women food writers experience these "positive connections to food." As US Americans' perceptions about women and work have changed over the last few decades, US American women's relationships with the kitchen and the food they prepare and eat have also changed. This book intends to celebrate the many ways in which women have returned to the space of the kitchen to write about the food that they prepare, eat, and enjoy.

1

DESIGN CHALLENGE

Better Homes and Gardens and the Changing Space of the US American Kitchen

In the May 1960 issue of *Better Homes and Gardens*, the magazine known for "the newest recipes, decorating ideas, and garden tips" ("*Better Homes and Gardens* Magazine"), the feature titled "Four Outstanding Family Homes" shows the relative insignificance of the space of the kitchen during this time period in US American history. This spread includes a two story, a split-level, a one level, and "A house that's ready to grow" (52). Each spread includes exterior and interior photographs of the home as well as the home's blueprints. While each house contains a kitchen in the design plans, the role that the kitchen plays in the features is not a major one. For instance, there are no photographs of the kitchen shown for either the split-level home or the house that's ready to grow. The two-story home does include photographs of the kitchen on the jump page, but the caption reads, "Presto, and the folding doors open to disclose a modern, fully equipped kitchen," indicating that the space is best closed off from view. The photographs of the one-level house show the combined kitchen and family room; the kitchen, however, is noticeably smaller; in fact, it's 9 feet by 14 feet, while the family room is 14½ feet by 18 feet. The remaining four homes all contain small kitchens: 10½ feet by 14 feet (two-story home), 12 feet by 8½ feet (split-level home), and 11½ feet by 13½ feet (the house that's ready to grow). By contrast, the living spaces of these homes, either the family room or living room, are significantly larger.

Over the last several decades, the middle-class US American kitchen has changed in both size and purpose, becoming more of a showpiece on the pages of home magazines and on home design television programs. Nino Sitchinava, principal economist at Houzz, "a website and online community about architecture, interior design and decorating, landscape design and home improvement," emphasizes the importance of the kitchen or what she describes as a "super kitchen" (HBS Dealer Staff). According to Sitchinava, "The modern 'super kitchen' supports family, friends and work and does it in style. . . . Our findings show that homeowners expect kitchen renovations to go far beyond improving flow, storage or aesthetics. The 'super kitchen' has literally become a living room, family room and office, with finishes, layouts and decor that challenge us to define where the kitchen ends and the rest of the home begins" (HBS Dealer Staff).

This contemporary representation of the kitchen is echoed in recent issues of *Better Home and Gardens*; kitchens are bigger and much more open. While *Better Homes and Gardens* magazine no longer includes blueprints, readers can visit the *Better Homes and Gardens* website to find house plans that fit their specifications. The blueprints for a home comparable in size to the two-story home featured in the 1960 issue showed a kitchen that was only slightly larger—approximately 11 feet by 14 feet—but entirely open to the activity room and dining area. This open concept trend is common in other homes searched on the site, and it is also reflected in the kitchens featured in the magazine.[1]

Since the 1960s, the physical space of the US American kitchen has been changing. Not only have the *Better Homes and Gardens'* kitchens grown in size and significance, but they have also changed in terms of function. In this chapter, I will examine the popular magazine *Better Homes and Gardens*—noting the way in which the magazine's representation of the space of the kitchen changed between 1960 and 2010. The magazine placed much more importance on the living spaces of the home, particularly the den or family room, and in blueprints for homes featured in the magazines, the kitchen was often positioned on the perimeter of the house, small and out of the way. Many post–World War II, middle- to upper-class, white US American women, the primary readership of the magazine, were already relegated to the home; they were then further marginalized by the placement and physical design of the kitchen. Conversely, by the early twenty-first century, the kitchen played a much more central role on the pages of the magazine; it is a larger, more open, and much more significant space. Most noteworthy, the magazine presents this space as one occupied by all members of the family. This reenvisioning of the space and purpose of the kitchen is important when considering the cultural context in which contemporary food memoirists are writing. As the physical space of the kitchen shifted, US American women, in turn, renegotiated their roles within that space, and US American women food writers speak to those changes in their work.

Architectural theorists have studied changes in home design, noting how various factors—from consumers' taste changes to advancements in technology—can influence building design.[2] Some of these scholars have addressed how historical circumstances, for example, the burgeoning middle class in the mid-twentieth century, might have affected the way in which architects think about form and function.[3] Others have reflected on the aesthetics of building, at times arguing for the inclusion of decorative elements and at other times demanding a minimalist approach to building design. The role that technology should play in building design is also a much debated topic among architectural theorists.

In *Sexuality and Space* (1992), Beatriz Colomina brilliantly summarizes a significant shift in architectural studies—a consideration of identity politics when it comes to building design.[4] She notes in her introduction that architectural theorists of the past have focused on "architecture as object," and she encourages readers to "abandon the traditional thought of architecture as object."[5] She continues, "Instead, architecture must be thought of as a system of representations in the same way that we think of drawings, photographs, models, film, or television, not only because the built object is made available to us through this media but because the built object is itself a system of representation."[6]

The most relevant theoretical work in relation to *Season to Taste* is the work that feminist architectural scholars have done, particularly in relation to the home.[7] In *Women Shaping Shelter, Technology, Consumption, and the Twentieth-Century House* (2004), Leslie N. Sharp echoes "[s]cholars such as Leslie Weisman, Angel Kwolek-Folland, and Daphne Spain[, who] have demonstrated how architectural design created gendered environments reinforcing traditional beliefs about the appropriate roles for men and women in society" (3). Because of these gendered environments—public/male, private/female—Lynne Walker argues that domestic space has historically been overlooked as a site of examination since "architects traditionally value the design of public buildings over private homes, the design of the building's exterior to its interior, and the building's structure to its decoration" (823).[8]

These "gendered spaces," as scholar Daphne Spain, professor and chair of the Department of Urban and Environmental Planning in the School of Architecture at the University of Virginia, deems them in her 1992 book of the same name, not only are inextricably linked to gendered behaviors but also can conspire to limit women's mobility. For example, Walker writes in "Home Making" about English architect Robert Kerr's houses. Kerr designed these spaces so that the rooms most associated with women were "placed at the back or . . . on the garden side of the house, protected from the street or the gaze of strangers" (826). By contrast, men's spaces were toward the front of the house, where they had easier access to the outside, or public, domain.

The kitchen is a particularly interesting site of examination when it comes to considering gender and home design. Throughout history, the kitchen was always a space primarily occupied by women; the women who inhabited this space may have been from various subject positions (from enslaved people to domestics to matriarchs of the house), but it was consistently a space designated female. In 2006, Louise C. Johnson, in "Browsing the Modern Kitchen: A Feast of Gender, Place, and Culture," recognizes the contributions that have been made to the study of the home: "One of the many contributions feminist scholars have made to the social sciences, has been to study and value domestic space" (123), but she also notes that specific locations within houses "especially the kitchen, tend to be considered infrequently by the spatial disciplines of planning, architecture and geography" (123).[9]

Two significant works that *do* examine this space are Ellen M. Plante's *The American Kitchen, 1700 to the Present: From Hearth to Highrise* (1995) and Elizabeth Collins Cromley's *The Food Axis: Cooking, Eating, and the Architecture of American Houses* (2010). Plante begins her study with the colonial kitchen and follows its development through the 1990s. Using such sources as period blueprints and advertisements, Plante discusses the ways in which the kitchen space transformed throughout the centuries—serving as the heart of the American home in the 1700s before moving to the rear of the first floor of the house in the 1870s and remaining there until the 1980s, when the US American family returned to a "multipurpose kitchen . . . reminiscent of the Colonial-era hall or keeping room" (267).

Likewise, architectural historian Elizabeth Collins Cromley chronologically examines the changing kitchen space from 1600 to 2010. Cromley coins the term "food axis," which refers to not just the space of the kitchen but any place within the home that is linked to food (e.g., cellar storage rooms or outdoor spaces or even other rooms in the home where eating occurs). Both Plante and Cromley reflect on the way in which architectural design often conspired to limit US American women's mobility.[10] For instance, Plante discusses how the domestic science movement of the early 1900s required women to heavily research domestic advice manuals in order to maintain a proper home—a movement that essentially kept women confined to this space. And, in *The Food Axis*, Cromley notes how in the 1970s architects such as the building firm Pearce and Pearce created homes that included a "command post" for the female head of household (201). The dining room spaces in these homes were not very large, but they did include a large family room that was open to the kitchen; consequently, the housewife could oversee the activities of her children while completing her tasks in the kitchen. While this change in building design opened up the space of the kitchen, Cromley notes that it also increased a woman's household duties; now, she had to cook dinner and oversee the children simultaneously. This particular change in building design and the associated shift in roles calls to mind Marjorie Hansen's term "superwoman syndrome" from her 1984 book of the same name. Not only were women of the 1970s and 1980s active in the workforce, but they also came home to be the chief operator of their household. Additionally, this floorplan still did not allow for a woman's full integration into the living spaces of the home.

Marginalizing the kitchen space within the already private sphere of the home further removed this space—and the women who performed their daily duties within it—from public life. As decades passed and women began to participate more in the public sphere, the space of the kitchen, as represented by home design magazines, became much bigger and more open to other rooms within the home. Women, as a result, became less isolated within the private space of the home, and since the kitchen was more accessible to other rooms in the house, its purpose shifted, becoming more than just a place to prepare meals. Rather, it served as a hub of family activity, a space occupied by not just by the matriarch but other members of the family as well. *Better Homes and Gardens* reflects these changes in kitchen design; as women's relationships with the public sphere broadened, the magazine's depictions of kitchens shifted as well in order to better suit their changing demographic.

Edwin Thomas Meredith launched *Better Homes and Gardens*, which was originally called *Fruit, Garden, and Home*, in 1922 (Reuss 7–8). The goal of his magazine was to target "the settled, middle-class American husband and wife whose primary interest were home and family" (G. Cooper 17). While there had been other publications with this same theme—such as *House Beautiful* and *House and Garden*—these magazines were aimed at "wealthy urban residents, not at the 'common' family" (17).

As Carol Reuss explains in her 1971 doctoral dissertation, *Better Homes and Gardens and Its Editors: An Historical Study from the Magazine's Founding to 1970*, although the editors of the magazine made occasional updates and small changes, they largely remained faithful to Meredith's initial core concept of the magazine—to be of service to the middle-class, white US American homemaker.[11] Today, *Better Homes and Gardens* maintains that initial mission; the 2018 media kit asserts, "Every issue of *Better Homes and Gardens* delivers smart, approachable editorial on design and individual style, decorating and gardening, food and entertaining, and person and family well-being" ("*Better Homes and Gardens*: Editorial Mission").[12]

While *Better Homes and Gardens* remained loyal to the magazine's original mission, the content was altered in order to keep up with popular US American trends. As a result, the depiction of the kitchen in *Better Homes and Gardens* shifted significantly from 1960 to 2010—the time period that I am focusing on specifically. In order to chronicle these changes, I looked at issues of *Better Homes and Gardens* from 1960, the height of the second wave feminist movement, through 2010, the height of the food memoir trend. I examined all twelve issues from the first year of each decade (1960, 1970, 1980, 1990, 2000, and 2010) to assess how significant the kitchen space was in relation to other areas of the home, to determine how much print space was devoted to kitchen design, and to consider what cultural messaging the magazine was deploying regarding both the purpose that space served and who occupies that space. As women became more actively involved in the public sphere, as the second wave feminist movement encouraged them to do, the kitchen space depicted on the pages of *Better Homes and Gardens* became more open, shifting from a space where meals were prepared by the female head of household to a hub of family life occupied by most members of the family.

In many issues of the magazine from 1960, there is not much emphasis on the space of the kitchen. Usually, the magazine focused on the living room or family room. For instance, the May 1960 issue included a design spread titled "Two Stories: More and Better Space." Here, photographs of the family room, dining room, living room, and the outdoor space were included. Instead, the emphasis was on the new technology available to female consumers. As historians such as Stephanie Coontz (*The Way We Never Were: American Families and the Nostalgia Trap*, 1992) and Laura Shapiro (*Something from the Oven: Reinventing Dinner in 1950s*, 2005) note, the 1950s were a period of time in which many US American women were leaving the factory jobs they had occupied during the war and returning to their homes. Companies focused on ways in which they could lessen these women's household "burdens" by developing and/or popularizing a variety of household goods—from packaged food to electric can openers. In the 1960 issues of *Better Homes and Gardens*, advertisements were included for such exciting products as a state-of-the-art dishwasher (Feb.), a Hotpoint fridge (Jul.), and a General Electric range (Oct.).

When the kitchen was featured during the 1960s, two things stood out—first, the size of the space and, second, the magazine's emphasis on the efficiency of the space. The kitchen was often small and closed off. Floor plans in three of the 1960 issues of the magazine included kitchen spaces that were 11½ by 13½, 10½ by 15½, and 12 by 8 feet.[13] To put this size in perspective, the largest kitchen of the three is the 96-square-foot kitchen. In 2016, *Kitchen and Bath* online reported, "The average size of a kitchen in newly-built single family

Better Homes and Gardens and the Changing Space of the Kitchen   29

homes is 161 sq. ft., just under 13 by 13 ft.," according to new research from the National Kitchen & Bath Association (NKBA)—65 feet larger ("NKBA Study Examines Average Kitchen Size in U.S.").[14]

The chief feature that the magazine focused on within this space was the kitchen's efficiency over style. In February 1960, the magazine included a four-page spread "An Exciting 'New' Traditional House!" The photograph of the kitchen showed a long, narrow room with cabinets at the end of the room as well as on the right side (a stovetop is included on that side as well). On the left side was a large brick wall with an oven built into it. The copy for the photograph reads, "Naturally nobody wants a completely traditional kitchen these days (what would you do with those big iron kettles!). But this kitchen combines an efficient U-shape and modern appliances with the heartiness of an old-fashioned brick wall" (55). Likewise, in August 1960, the author of "It's the Same Size—But BIGGER" wrote, "A woman who values cooking time, as I do, hankers for a kitchen fully armed with tools in their own, neat, handy place. My old kitchen fell short of that dream" (92). In order to fix this kitchen space, they needed to figure out "[h]ow to fit everything in so little space" (92). The result was "this new, convenient, storage-packed kitchen—and all in the same small 8 × 10 space." In May 1960, there was an article that featured a kitchen with folding doors that, when closed, would literally hide the kitchen from view. When open, there was a "modern, fully equipped kitchen" (120). In this case, the kitchen was unobtrusive yet extremely efficient.

As in the 1960s, technological advancements and efficiency were also emphasized in regard to kitchens in the 1970s. In the January 1970 issue, an advertisement for "The Counter that Cooks by Corning" declared that their product would replace the "old-fashioned range top" (31). Issues from the 1970s also included small kitchen spaces. In January 1970, three houses were featured; the dimensions for the kitchen spaces were 10 by 10½ (37), 8 by 8½ (39), and 8 by 8 (41). Not only were the spaces smaller, but the amount of print space devoted to these spaces was equally insignificant. The photographs included for two of the three houses mentioned above include small corner photographs of the kitchen, while there is no photograph of the kitchen from the third house.

These messages about the marginalization of the kitchen space were often repeated in the text for the magazine, as the magazine continued to promote kitchens that were physically separated from the home's entertaining spaces. While the magazine occasionally mentioned the opening up of a space, more often than not, that opening up was tempered by some sort of partition. For instance, the copy for a spread titled "Three Kitchens Where the Action Is" in the April 1970 issue notes, "This compact kitchen acts twice its size with an 18-inch-wide buffet/bar to back it up. Plastic panels close while guests serve themselves" (Z24). In the May 1970 issue, there is a photograph that accompanies the article "New Space for Family Living." The photograph features the informal dining area of the home in the foreground with a pony wall with decorated columns on top that act as a divider between the eating area and food preparation space (73).

In the 1980s, however, the magazine devoted much more print space to the kitchen. In fact, in February 1980, the table of contents featured a section titled "Kitchens."[15] And, when kitchens were featured, there were often several pages dedicated to them. For instance, the February issue included a five-page layout titled "Idea Kitchen" (37–41), April included two features on kitchens "Revive an Old House" and "Making a Small Kitchen Work Big," June included two kitchen features, and the November edition included an eight-page spread titled "Open Plan Kitchen with Out-of-Sight Storage" (46+). The August edition even mentioned a kitchen remodel on the magazine's cover.

During this decade, *Better Homes and Gardens* also began to entertain the idea of the open concept kitchen that would become so popular in later years.[16] For instance, in the April 1980 article "Making a Small Kitchen Work Big," the small kitchen "problem" was solved by "[removing] the partition between the kitchen and breakfast nook." Not only did the magazine emphasize a kitchen space that was open to other areas of the home, but it also highlighted how the kitchen size could increase if walls were taken down.

In the subsequent decades, 1990s, 2000s, and 2010s, the magazine continued to promote a more open concept kitchen and advocate for a larger the kitchen. To determine these changes, I closely examined the January issues from these decades as well as the September issues.[17] Size-wise, the January and September issues from the 1990s, as well as the other issues from that year, did not include floorplans with square footage marked. However, in the January 1990 edition, there is a note in the "Perfect-for-Parties Kitchen" article that "[t]he new kitchen space and sitting room bump-out are open to each other and the outside patio, for a non-stop living area about 50 feet long" (66). In 2000, the kitchen featured in the January issue was 12 by 14 feet (111), while the September issue included a 12- by 10-foot kitchen. In the January 2010 issues, a kitchen featured was 16 by 12 feet (47). When comparing the square footage of these kitchens to the square footage from the 1960s issues (11½ by 13½, 10½ by 15½, and 12 by 8), there is a noticeable increase in home space allotted for the kitchen. And this space was not closed off; rather, it opened up to other areas of the home. The accompanying text to "Perfect-for-Parties Kitchen" emphasizes the "non-stop living area." Likewise, the blueprints for the kitchens featured in the January 2000 and January 2010 issues both open up to other rooms—the family room and an area labeled sitting, respectively.

Print space devoted to the kitchen increased as well. To start, the January 1990 issue contained only one feature about the kitchen, while in September 1990, there were two kitchens featured. In January 2000, one of the two renovations honored in the home remodel contest featured a kitchen.[18] The September 2000 issue showed an extremely significant increase in kitchen coverage. There was a feature on "Neat Nooks," which included a command center design in the kitchen (60); a feature on "Cook Centers," which showcased prep areas in four different kitchens—"One-Stop

Stir-Fry," "Pasta Perfect," "Pizza, Pretzels, and Pastry," and "Room for Recipes Galore." There was also a small shot of a kitchen for the spread "Farm Fresh" and a two-page display of a kitchen in "Remarkable Renovation." The issues from 2010 were no different. Three kitchens were featured in January, and five kitchens were featured in September.

In reviewing these issues, it became clear that as time passed the kitchen became a much more significant feature in *Better Homes and Gardens*. In fact, in the September 2000 issue, the magazine advertised the "Intelligent Kitchen Tour at the Mall":

> Coming soon to a mall near you! A special video preview of the Intelligent Kitchen—the kitchen of tomorrow that's available today—from *Better Homes and Gardens* magazine. Get a sneak peek at what's in store for kitchens in the 21st century by visiting this state-of-the-art design via big-screen TV monitors and checking out the latest in high-tech appliances, low maintenance finishes, and easy-living features. As the production's camera pans across each area and zooms in for close ups, you'll see how our trend-setting kitchen fits the lifestyles of families just like yours. (54)

This display includes dates and locations for twelve different participating malls where the Intelligent Kitchen would be featured. The accompanying drawing shows a home space with the following labels: work area, beverage center, dining, hearth area, office, and laundry. This "kitchen of tomorrow" is very much in line with Sitchinava's description of the "super kitchen." With spaces such as the hearth area and laundry area, the Intelligent Kitchen, like the super kitchen, challenges notions of "where the kitchen ends and the rest of the home begins."

More significantly, there was a shift in who was imagined in the space of the kitchen. No longer was the kitchen space marginalized; rather, it served as the anchor of the home—a place where family members, both male and female, gathered.[19] In early editions of the

Better Homes and Gardens and the Changing Space of the Kitchen 33

magazine, writers used either purely descriptive language regarding the space or directly addressed the presumed female reader by using "you." Such examples of descriptive language are "The door beyond leads to the generous utility room" (February 1960, 90), "White load-bearing posts accent the practical plywood siding on the exterior" (Mar. 1960, 64), and "Since family living is at the rear of this house, there's no need for an old-fashioned, enclosed front porch" (May 1960, 120). Copy such as "Naturally nobody wants a completely traditional kitchen these days (what would you do with those big iron kettles!)" (February 1960, 55) and "This split-level home is put together with your family in mind" (May 1960, 56) directly addresses the reader. As mentioned earlier, while the magazine was marketed to both male and female readers (the US American family), in both cases the "you" mentioned here is most likely gendered female since it was the female head of household who historically occupied (and was represented on the pages of the magazine as occupying) the home space.

In later decades, as the space of the kitchen opened up, so did expectations about who would occupy the space. Instead of the presumed female "you," there was much more emphasis on couples working together in the space or on families enjoying the space with one another. Text accompanying a special advertising section for the February 1990 encapsulates the kitchen's changing purpose: "On country farm, or in city brownstone, it's the heart of the house. The scene for solo late-night forays, for boisterous gatherings of the clan, for casual morning coffee with friends, and elaborate preparations for the ultimate evening meal." Later in that issue, we see a similar sentiment in the article "Kitchens with Style": "This is a kitchen for long afternoons, a magnet for family and friends. Light pours in through abundant windows and French doors. Built-out walls and a gently curved soffit ease the refrigerator and cabinets into the background. Refinished chairs and an antique table-turned-island complete the family room feeling. Come in and sit a spell. You can almost smell the fresh-baked apple pie" (78). This second quote contains the use of the personal pronoun "you," but the "you" seems more ambiguous—less specifically gendered as in earlier issues. "You" is not specifically the maker of the food; rather, the "you" in this scenario is the one who experiences pleasure from the smell.

From 2000 on, the emphasis shifts to family enjoyment. For instance, in January 2000, "[a] passion for cooking led Cynthia and Jack Dekker of Littleton, Colorado, to totally retool their 1960s kitchen. 'We also wanted room for our children to take part in meal preparation,' says Cynthia" (110). In March 2010—for a special section on "Life in the Kitchen," the introductory quote reads, "Big or small, the kitchen is our best-loved space for making meals and memories. This month: easy ways to bring yours more comfort, style, and function" (31). And, in the April 2010 article "Reality Check," Jenny and Joe Keenan's house is featured with the following description of their kitchen, "Everything happens in this one area. When she's scraping Play-Doh off the kitchen island or her husband, Joe, is flipping the Saturday morning pancakes, they can still keep tabs on the kids coloring or rummaging through a basket" (38); each member of the household has a role to play in this home space. Additionally, this sense of family enjoyment of this space is also highlighted in many of the pull quotes from articles featured in issues during these decades. In May 1990, a pull quote that accompanied the feature "From Dowdy to Dynamite" reads, "This design brings our guests easily into the kitchen to watch, help out, or whatever" (54). In March 2010, a pull quote included in the special section "The kitchen is the center of life in the house, and it's a gathering place for the neighborhood" (34). Not only is this space the heart of the house, easily accessed by all members of the family, but it has also opened up to individuals outside the home. While earlier issues of the magazine centered the US American housewife in the space of the kitchen, at the beginning of the twenty-first century, the matriarch of the home is no longer the sole occupant of the space.

The *Better Homes and Gardens* September 2010 issue contains the spread "Then Again." In it, Denise Gee and Rob Brinson profile

Better Homes and Gardens and the Changing Space of the Kitchen   35

homeowners Mila Goldman-Moore and Waco Moore, who live in a home showcased in the September 1957 issue as "*Better Homes and Gardens* Idea Home of the Year" (49). The 2010 feature focuses on the ways in which the house has held up over time, consistently emphasizing how forward thinking the design in 1957 had been. As Goldman-Moore notes, "At the time this house was built, architecture was just starting to promote the idea of family time. . . . Lucky for us, it still does that perfectly" (81).

The house, in terms of design, has not changed all that much. The kitchen is between the living and family rooms (50), and the original measurements of each space are 13½ by 9½, 20 by 15, and 14½ by 15 feet, respectively. While the 2010 issue does not include measurements in its featured blueprint, the author of the piece notes that the only significant change made to the house was to knock out a partition between the master bedroom and dressing area. In 1957, the kitchen was described as such: "Corridor kitchen has direct route for serving family room, living room, porch, and outdoors" (56). The homeowners in 2010 note that they have not yet remodeled the kitchen because they are still thinking about the best way to improve it. Its footprint, then, has not been altered.

What has shifted dramatically in the contemporary spread is who is represented in the home space. In the 2010 feature, there are seven images included. Two feature interior shots with no occupants; a third features the couple's daughter, Jette, in her space. The very first image features the father and daughter riding a bike outside the house while the mother waits near the house; a later image features the mother and daughter in the master bedroom. The final two images are the most interesting: the living room shows the father and daughter enjoying time together while the kitchen shot features the father alone, cooking. It is important to note that there are no images of the mother alone in the home. By contrast, the 1957 issue features twenty images of the idea home. These images are scenes both inside and outside of the home. Of the twenty images, twelve depict women in the home (either the daughter or mother alone or together) while six depict men (either the son or father alone or together).[20] The only interior shot in which the father is included is in the living room with the two children.

The messaging of these two spreads clearly shows the way in which the space of the kitchen has shifted in regard to occupation. Visually, the 1957 issue makes clear that women are associated with homemaking tasks such as cooking, serving, and sewing. By contrast, the 2010 issue imagines the male head of household as an equal occupant in the kitchen space, independently preparing food for his daughter. *Better Homes and Gardens'* representation of the kitchen space in terms of size, location, placement, *and* who occupies it shifted considerably over the decades, contributing to a reimagining of the physical space of the kitchen and its meaning for women. This historical context is meaningful as I explore, in subsequent chapters, how food memoirists write about contemporary kitchen space and consider who inhabits the space and how they negotiate and write about their relationships with the preparation and consumption of food.

2

"A WOMAN'S MOST REWARDING WAY OF LIFE"

The Feminist/Housewife Debate and Contemporary Women's Response

In 2009, Ruth Reichl, author of such food memoirs as *Tender at the Bone: Growing Up at the Table* (1998), *Comfort Me with Apples: More Adventures at the Table* (2001), and *Garlic and Sapphires: The Secret Life of a Critic in Disguise* (2005), published a book titled *Not Becoming My Mother: And Other Things She Taught Me along the Way* (2009).[1] In it, she declared, "My mother was a great example of everything I didn't want to be" (7). Upon her mother's death, Reichl spent time going through her mother's diaries and letters. What she found revealed not only her mother's frustration, but it also reflected the sentiments of many white, heterosexual, middle-class US American women of her mother's generation.[2] Reichl describes these women, housewives of the post–World War II era, as educated but bored; they were discouraged from establishing careers, and the availability of "labor-saving devices" reduced the amount of time that women needed to spend caring for their families and homes (9). Her description brings to mind the women Betty Friedan interviewed for *The Feminine Mystique* (1963)—women suffering from what Friedan called "the problem that has no name" (57). *Not Becoming My Mother* becomes Reichl's attempt to make sense of her mother's fate, interrogating how historical circumstances may have contributed to the shaping of her mother's life and the lives of so many other women like her at the time.

It is clear in reading Reichl's memoir and Reichl's work as a whole that Reichl distanced herself from the role that so many of her mother's generation occupied. Unlike her mother, who spent most of her time in the private sphere of the home taking care of her husband and family, Reichl entered eagerly into the public sphere, taking on workplace challenges as they presented themselves. She served as the *Los Angeles Times* restaurant critic and food editor (1984–1993), the *New York Times* restaurant critic (1993–1999), and *Gourmet* magazine's editor-in-chief (1999–2009). According to the biography on her author page, she has produced the four memoirs mentioned above, two cookbooks, and a novel; she has also contributed to a variety of food collections. Her speech upon receiving a 2008 Matrix Award is included in *Not Becoming My Mother*; in it, Reichl concludes, "And so today, when people ask, 'Why do you work so hard?' I think of my mother, who was not allowed to do it, and say, 'Because I can'" (10).[3]

Reichl's quest to define herself as different from her mother and the women of her mother's generation is reflective of a larger tendency for women of the second wave feminist movement to distance themselves from the roles occupied by the previous generation of women. As Stacy Gillis and Joanne Hollows assert in the opening of their introduction to *Feminism, Domesticity, and Popular Culture* (2009): "The relationship between second wave feminism and domesticity was frequently troubled. Since the publication of Betty Friedan's *The Feminine Mystique* in 1963, the idea that an investment in domestic life is contrary to the aims of feminism has structured much feminist debate and the figure most closely

The Feminist/Housewife Debate and Women's Response 39

associated with the domestic—the housewife—often operates as the feminist's 'other'" (1). As Hollows notes in *Domestic Cultures* (2008), women of the time period often saw these "gendered spheres" as "reproducing gender inequalities—indeed, some suggest, that this is even the root cause of women's oppression" (54). As a result, the discourse of the second wave feminist movement, which largely focused on the concerns of middle-class, white, heterosexual US American women, often encouraged these women to move beyond the private sphere of the home and into the public sphere of the workplace. The physical space of the kitchen, which, as we have seen in the previous chapter, marginalized women within the home, became a contested site—a symbol of women's oppression.

Reichl's food writing, from her earliest publication *Mmmmm: A Feastiary* (1972) to her most recent memoir, *Save Me the Plums* (2019), serves as a touchstone for the changing gender politics associated with the kitchen. In this chapter, I will examine Reichl's memoir *Comfort Me with Apples: More Adventures at the Table*. While published during the early twenty-first century, the memoir focuses on Reichl's experiences in the late 1970s as she rises to food-writing fame from her position as a restaurant critic at *New West* magazine to her work for the *Los Angeles Times* as a restaurant critic and food editor. I argue that Reichl—in the spirit of second wave feminist discourse—strives to clearly establish herself as a professional, aligning her text with the literary tradition of the memoir rather than that of the cookbook. I will return to Reichl's later works in my afterword. Reichl's oeuvre spans several decades, and her shift in thinking about women's relationships with the kitchen and home cooking—particularly in her most recent work, her novel *Delicious!* (2014) and *My Kitchen Year: 136 Recipes That Saved My Life* (2015)—speaks to these larger shifts in cultural consciousness about women, the space of the kitchen, and the preparation and enjoyment of food. Over the course of her career, Reichl resolves for herself some of the historical tensions between home/work, private/public, and housewife/feminist.

Reichl published two works prior to the publication of *Comfort Me with Apples*. Her earliest foray into food writing came with her 1972 publication of *Mmmmm: A Feastiary*, and she followed this work up with the food memoir *Tender at the Bone: Growing Up at the Table* (1998). In both texts, Reichl resists characterizing herself as a home cook. Although Reichl, on her website, describes *Mmmmm: A Feastiary* as a cookbook, it is an interesting take on this traditional text. The book offers recipes, musings about food, and avant-garde illustrations, collages, and photographs contributed by artists such as Reichl's husband at the time, Doug Hollis. In *Tender at the Bone*, Reichl chronicles a number of food-inspired stories from her childhood to the early days of her marriage and pairs those stories with recipes. The most memorable story from this collection is a story in which Reichl's mother, cooking for a combined UNICEF fundraiser and engagement party for Reichl's brother, unintentionally gives twenty-six guests food poisoning. These stories of her mother's horrible cooking erase the nostalgia often associated with home-cooked, childhood meals.

Comfort Me with Apples presents the most sustained and compelling meditation on the public/private divisions of the time period. In this memoir, Reichl responds to the images of what was called "the happy housewife heroine" presented to the women of her mother's generation. As cultural critics have noted, the image presented by popular culture mediums of the postwar period, particularly advertising, "was that of the ideal homemaker, epitomized by . . . icons such as June Cleaver and Donna Reed" (C. Smith 107). In her book *Something from the Oven: Reinventing Dinner in 1950s America* (2005), Laura Shapiro relates the perfect example of a model postwar housewife when she describes the opening sequence to *The Betty Crocker Show*, which aired in the fall of 1950:

> A long, loving shot of the General Mills flag rippling in the breeze opened the show, and then the scene shifted to an inspirational tableau vivant. A young woman posed outdoors on a promontory

against the sky, two small children clinging to her hands. Her chin was lifted, her gaze was unflinching, and her purpose was grave. As she paused with her little brood on their arduous journey, the announcer made it clear just what she symbolized. "Homemaking," he intoned. "A woman's most rewarding way of life." (192)

Shapiro's description reveals the popular image of women that was valued at the time period by television executives and advertisers. This visual of the middle-class, white US American homemaker woman and her children implicitly conveys the message of the commercial, and if the audience fails to pick up on that message, the announcer's explicit declaration should erase any confusion. Consistently, women of the era were confronted with these images, left to measure their own lives against an impossibly high standard set for them.

In *The Feminine Mystique* (1963), Betty Friedan examined the impact that these images had on US American women. She interviewed middle-class white US American women of the era (women of Reichl's mother's generation) and determined that they were suffering from "the problem that has no name"—a feeling of great unhappiness despite the nation's economic prosperity and stability. To combat this feeling, Friedan encouraged US American housewives to return to the public sphere as a way for women to overcome their discontent. In her concluding chapter, "A New Life Plan for Women," she writes "The only way for a woman, as for a man, to find herself, to know herself as a person, is by creative work of her own" (472); in other words, she writes in order for a woman "to realize her abilities fully, to achieve identity in society in a life plan that can encompass marriage and motherhood, is . . . the lifelong commitment to art or science, to politics or profession" (476).

In the opening chapter of *Comfort Me with Apples*, Reichl immediately establishes the polarization of the feminist and housewife when she relates the story of accepting a job as a restaurant critic for *New West* magazine. Reichl, who lives in what she deems "the

People's Republic of Berkeley" (6), recognizes that her taking such a job would immediately align her with that of the establishment in the eyes of her friends and family. One of her housemates in the Berkeley housing cooperative (Changing Way) in which she lives even questions her: "You're going to spend your life telling spoiled, rich people where to eat too much obscene food?" (6). His incredulity encapsulates their concerns.

While these concerns about socioeconomic class and meaningful work might be considered progressive politics, Reichl's housemates' and her husband's views on gender equality are very much entrenched in rather outdated expectations regarding women's roles. Reichl explains that on Channing Way she is often the one responsible for preparing meals and cleaning up. When Reichl shares the news of her new job with Doug, he acknowledges that her skills should be rewarded but immediately follows his praise with, "But you don't have to say yes. . . . Why don't you stop working? I'm making enough money now. You could quit the restaurant, give up magazine work, and stay home and write" (7–8). While Reichl does indicate that Doug's grand plan for her includes writing, her recollection begins with all that she would have to give up. Even Reichl's parents express their disappointment at her career choice. Her mother, when told, is concerned that Reichl will never "move out of that ridiculous commune, settle down, and have a family" (9). Reichl recalls being surrounded by individuals whose expectations for her life are not consistent with her own aspirations.

In her first chapter, "The Other Side of the Bridge," Reichl expresses the frustration she feels at having "always been the ultimate good girl" (9) and relates her first significant act of rebellion against that image. She writes, "I was thirty years old and I had spent my whole life pleasing other people. Although I lived in a commune, I was married to a man my parents loved, called my mother every day, and spent most of my time cooking the meals and cleaning up the house" (9). Reichl's description of herself comes dangerously close to Friedan's "happy housewife heroine"—the woman,

The Feminist/Housewife Debate and Women's Response   43

painted by women's magazines, who is "young and frivolous, almost childlike; fluffy and feminine; passive; gaily content in the world of bedroom and kitchen, sex, babies, and home" (83). In recognizing what she is in danger of becoming, Reichl begins to rebel; her first act of defiance comes—crab cakes.

A series of unfortunate events lead up to this meal. The day before this meal Reichl meets up with her *New West* editor, Colman Andrews. As noted earlier, her friends and family disapprove of this career choice. The day of the meal Reichl awakens to "the sour smell of spilled wine . . . the kitchen table lined with peanut shells and crumpled napkins: dirty plates . . . piled high in the sink. Used coffee grounds, looking horrifyingly like ants, spilled crazily across the counter" (22). Reichl realizes that the expectation is for her to clean up the mess, and she finds herself getting increasingly agitated by this fact. As she is "jabbing angrily at the dishes" she washes (22), a housemate expresses concern at her plan to cook her scrambled eggs in butter, having just read an article about how butter is problematic. Then, Doug calls and indicates that he has no intention of settling down on Channing Way but instead intends to continue to travel and create art. Upset, Reichl seeks solace in the kitchen.

However, the meal that she cooks—crab cakes—is not a traditional "comfort food." More significantly, it is an extravagance that her housemates and husband will surely disapprove of. She writes in the preface to the recipe, "But this time I was making more than a meal. I was cooking in shorthand, sending a message to myself. Just look at this list of ingredients! Crabmeat, a true luxury, was definitely not on the Channing Way list of approved foods. For that reason, I found the sizzle each time a crab cake hit the butter in the pan profoundly satisfying" (24). Reichl is resentful of the fact that she is the one expected to cook and clean, and she is frustrated that her housemates are not taking her entrance into the professional world seriously. She is also profoundly disappointed that her husband does not value her professional interests as much as he values his own. She lashes out, cooking a meal that includes ingredients that fly in the face of their ideals. Cooking in this moment is her act of rebellion—against her role as caretaker of the home on Channing Way and against her being confined to the space of the home while Doug travels for his career.

Reichl finds the outdated gender expectations that pervade Channing Way to be present in the male-dominated field of the restaurant industry. Reichl encounters many men who, upon meeting her, expect her to be something other than she is. For instance, upon walking into Michael McCarty's under-construction restaurant in Santa Monica, chef Jonathan Waxman tells her, "We're not hiring waitresses yet" (67). Later, she recounts a story about chef Bruce Cost, who has been invited to cook Asian food for a select group of people in Berkeley. Cost spends the whole evening ordering Reichl around, having her serve the food, not realizing that she's the reporter sent to interview him. When she visits China to produce a piece for *Metropolitan Home,* her tour guide labels her "a troublesome girl" (123) and is concerned with her tendency to fraternize with "private citizens" (122), her sleeveless tops, and her "not wearing anything to hold up [her] breasts" (123). The outdated expectations that her housemates and husband have regarding a woman's place in the world are not much different from the expectations she encounters in the professional world.

In response, Reichl centers her narrative on stories of her professional success. This emphasis calls to mind the organizing principle for the discourse of the second wave feminist movement—moving beyond the private sphere of the home. The National Organization for Women (NOW), a US American feminist organization founded in 1966, supported this rejection of the private sphere for the public in their 1966 Statement of Purpose. Written by Friedan, the Statement of Purpose, which can be found on NOW's website, asserts, "The purpose of NOW is to take action to bring women into full participation in the mainstream of US American society now, exercising all the privileges and responsibilities thereof in truly equal partnership with men." The Statement of Purpose deals

The Feminist/Housewife Debate and Women's Response   45

directly with the struggles of homemakers: "WE REJECT the current assumptions that a man must carry the sole burden of supporting himself, his wife, and family, and that a woman is automatically titled to lifelong support by a man upon her marriage, or that marriage, home and family are primarily woman's world and responsibility— hers, to dominate—his to support." NOW's Statement of Purpose makes clear, as Friedan did in her earlier work, that engagement with the public sphere can and should be expected of middle- to upper-class, white US American women. Ultimately, it is not in the home where women belong but "as part of the decision-making mainstream of American political, economic and social life" ("The National Organization for Women's 1966 Statement of Purpose").

Second wave feminist writer and political activist Meredith Tax crystallizes this idea in the song that she wrote "There Was a Young Woman Who Swallowed a Lie."[4] Here, Tax begins with the phrase, "There was a young woman who swallowed a lie." The accompanying illustration shows a woman, mouth open, with the words "Woman's place is in the home" being ingested. The song goes on to detail the progression of this woman's life, her meeting a man, her getting married, her having children. The text included on each panel ends with the opening phrase of the song—"We all know why she swallowed that lie"—referencing that original falsehood that women should remain inside the home. For Tax, this lie is at the root of all this woman's eventual problems as she shows in her accompanying illustrations. It prompts her consumption of beauty products ("lipstick & candy & powder & puff"); it fuels her desire to find a man, no matter how sexist he may be ("I like 'em dumb, baby, you suit me just fine"); and it results in her desperately consulting Dr. Spock's childcare book in the hopes of reining in her four monstrous children. Tax's poem closes with the woman's realization that the lie is just that—a lie—and the concluding panel of Tax's poem shows the woman running toward four other women who are seated under a banner that reads, "SISTERHOOD IS POWERFUL!!" For Tax, and many women activists in the 1960s,

46   The Feminist/Housewife Debate and Women's Response

the only way for women to progress is to literally exchange the role of housewife for the role of feminist.

Reichl's self-characterization in these moments as a bra-burning rabble-rouser is interesting in light of her earlier characterization as "the ultimate good girl." While Reichl's recollections acknowledge the difficulties that she faced breaking into the restaurant industry, her narrative ultimately highlights her triumphs—not the obstacles—within the public sphere. For instance, her story about how chef Bruce Cost reveals his own gender biases by mistaking Reichl for a waitress ultimately puts Reichl in the position of power. After all, she is able to witness firsthand his preparation of "sesame-crusted deep-fried shrimp toasts" and "quail eggs" in a way that she would not have been able to if she had been seated outside with other guests.[5] Each of these encounters ends with Reichl publishing a significant food piece—whether it be about the opening of McCarty's restaurant for *New West*, the meal that Cost cooked for Alice Waters and her friends, or the culinary treasures that a newly opened China has to offer.[6] Though Reichl acknowledges facing professional challenges, she writes of the ways that she successfully navigates them and becomes the author of her own tale, ultimately controlling her own image and emphasizing those traits she possesses that stand in opposition to Friedan's "happy housewife heroine." Consistently, as readers, we learn through Reichl's writing that she has a strong engagement with personal success and the professional world.

Interestingly enough, Reichl segments her narrative with separate storylines about her work and her marriage. On one hand, Reichl records her rise to fame as a food writer, hobnobbing with the likes of Wolfgang Puck, yet on the other hand, she shares the story of her failing marriage to successful sound sculptor and landscape artist Doug Hollis. These parallel narratives become even more distinct when Reichl begins an affair with her editor Colman Andrews. Taking up with Andrews, her immediate superior and her eventual mentor, is significant in regard to Reichl's separation of home and work life. Though an affair is certainly personal, in Reichl's case, her involvement with Andrews is very much professionally tied. Each of their meetings revolves around food and is, largely, part of Reichl's informal education as a food critic. Additionally, the secretive nature of their affair (Reichl's friends, her family, and, of course, her husband do not know about it) further dissociates Reichl's homelife on Channing Way from her professional life. When Reichl and Andrews rendezvous, they do so outside of Berkeley, meeting first in Los Angeles, spending time in Paris, and then continuing to meet in Los Angeles. This geographical separation underscores the distinction between Reichl's public and private spheres. Reichl's engagement with Andrews and the restaurant industry is far removed from her life on Channing Way, where she waits for her husband to return from his various artistic endeavors. This dual narrative approach reinforces, then, the professional/personal, feminist/housewife binary that pervades Reichl's text.

Reichl's recipes, which are included at the end of each chapter, also highlight her engagement with the public sphere. Reichl concludes most chapters with a recipe or recipes that are clearly demarcated from the narrative proper. There are no asides within the narrative that reference the recipe directly. While the recipes that conclude each chapter serve as a way to reinforce that chapter's central theme, they are often loosely connected to the primary narrative. The majority of these recipes are aligned with restaurant food rather than home cooking. The recipes that Reichl includes are rather sophisticated, requiring multiple steps and some previous cooking know-how. Many of these recipes include notations that address the recipe's complexities. For instance, in her "Fried Capers and Calves' Brains with Sherry Butter Sauce," she notes, "The brains are almost entirely texture—like savory marshmallows in a crisp crust. . . . They're a lot of work, but they're worth it" (297); and in another, for "Danny's Lemon Pasta" (255), she indicates, "It took me a long time to perfect this recipe" (255). On the whole, the recipes that Reichl includes evoke the professional kitchen rather than the home kitchen.

Reichl most obviously positions her food as restaurant fare when she references famous restaurants and/or chefs in her recipes. For instance, she includes the recipe "La Vieille Maison Soup" for Robert Charles's "variation on the classic French onion soup" (100); the title of the recipe references Charles's successful garlic restaurant in Truckee, California. Her recipe for "Grilled California Goat Cheese on Toast" includes the note "This is an adaptation of the appetizer Wolfgang Puck served at the White House during the economic summit of 1983" (236). She also includes Puck's recipe for "Chinois Curried Oysters with Cucumber Sauce and Salmon Roe" (237) along with Michael McCarty's recipe for pasta and scallops, which she titles "Michael's Pasta and Scallops" (80–81)—no last name needed. Consistently, with the selection of recipes for her memoir, Reichl firmly writes herself out of the private kitchen of the home and into the public kitchens of the restaurant world.

Reichl began her professional food-writing career in the 1970s; today, she continues to write, having published a novel (*Delicious!* 2014), a cookbook (*My Kitchen Year: 136 Recipes That Saved My Life*, 2015), and most recently a memoir about her experiences working for *Gourmet* magazine (*Save Me the Plums*, 2019). Her career, then, becomes an interesting touchstone for exploring women's relationships with food preparation and the home kitchen, and I will return to Reichl's more recent work in my afterword. While Reichl clearly positions herself in the public kitchens of the restaurant world in her earlier work, her more recent work, like the contemporary food memoirs I will examine in the subsequent chapters, reflects a rejection of the binary of public/private and explores a more nuanced relationship between her and the food that she prepares and consumes.

3

WINKING WHILE WE BAKE

Recoding Kitchen Space
in Contemporary Food Writing

During the 1992 race for the Democratic ticket, presidential hopeful Jerry Brown accused his opponent, Bill Clinton, of "funneling money to his wife's law firm for state business" (Berke). The media firestorm that followed the debate was intense—but not for the reasons you might suspect. While there was attention focused on Brown's accusation, the media and the public, it seemed, were more focused on Hillary Clinton's response. During questioning about her law firm's dealings, Hillary made the controversial comment, "I suppose I could have stayed at home, baked cookies and had teas, but what I decided was to fulfill my profession, which I entered before my husband was in public life" (Lauter).

Clinton's statement was not taken well. It "reportedly provoked more angry calls to the . . . campaign than had a controversy over Clinton's Vietnam era draft record" ("Brown Takes Second Place in Michigan"). Many read these remarks as disparaging to homemakers; some called her "an elitist and an ultra-feminist" ("Making Hillary Clinton an Issue"). There was retaliation. The *Washington*

Times reported that those outraged by Hillary's comments had been sending cookies by the dozens to the governor's office in Arkansas; the newspaper conveniently included that address for their readers (Elvin). ABC News' late-night television news program *Nightline* aired a segment titled "Making Hillary Clinton an Issue," where people such as author Patricia O'Brien and University of Southern California law professor Susan Estrich discussed the changing role of first ladies throughout history, why the public had such a strong response to Hillary's statement, and the potential liability that she presented for her husband's campaign. And *Family Circle* even got into the action, announcing in their 21 July 1992 issue a bipartisan bake-off (Jaworski 9). They published two recipes for chocolate chip cookies—Clinton's and Barbara Bush's. Readers were invited to bake both, decide which was better, and send their votes on a postcard to the magazine. Interestingly enough, in the November issue, it was announced that Clinton won with 55.2 percent of the vote.

Kim Severson, in her 2010 memoir *Spoon Fed: How Eight Cooks Saved My Life*, shares her reaction to "the Clinton cookie incident." Her response to this event—nearly twenty years later—puts a slightly different spin on the situation. While Severson acknowledges the sexist overtones of the "scandal," she also writes in her introduction, "The thing that bothered me most about the cookie incident wasn't the inherent sexism. It was that Hillary acted like giving out a good cookie recipe diminished her" (5). Severson continues, noting, "Having mastery of the art of cookie baking should not make one less of a person" and, in fact, she "want[s] a leader who is thoughtful about these kinds of things" (6). Severson's analysis of the incident is more puzzled than outraged, as she wonders why Clinton assumes that being able to cook weakens her power, for, to Severson, "food is power" (6).

Severson's 2010 response to the Clinton-Bush bake-off is representative of a gradual shift in the US American public's consciousness regarding women and the kitchen. At the time, the popular press—and Clinton herself—still saw the role of homemaker and career-minded woman to be at odds. Yet, nearly two decades later, Kim Severson questions why a career-minded woman and a baker of cookies need to be two mutually exclusive roles. Rather than seeing the space of the kitchen as antagonistic—imprisoning the cook within the private sphere—Severson, in her memoir, sees it as a place of liberation, enabling her to self-actualize as a writer, a lesbian, a wife, and eventually a mother.

As we saw in the previous chapter, discourse from the second wave feminist movement often positioned the private/public and housewife/feminist at odds with one another. Contemporary women food writers such as Severson, however, often reject the binaries upheld by second wave feminist rhetoric. In this chapter, I argue that these contemporary writers are recoding the space of the kitchen, updating the image of the home cook.[1] I will examine the rhetorical strategies deployed by third wave feminist publications such as *Bitch* and *BUST*, looking more specifically at the way in which those strategies are applied to the space of the home. Unlike second wave feminist rhetoric, which characterized the home as a place of imprisonment, these third wave publications, I argue, reimagine the space of the home as a place of enjoyment and even liberation. Women engaged in domestic arts, such as cooking, often do so because it is a gratifying pastime—and, for some, a professional outlet.

The primary focus of this chapter is on the work of food blogger Jocelyn Delk Adams, who engages the tensions of past and present food work in compelling ways. On her blog (*Grandbaby Cakes*) and in her cookbook (*Grandbaby Cakes: Modern Recipes, Vintage Charm, Soulful Memories*, 2015), Delk Adams explores her own relationship with the kitchen and her role within that space. She adopts the persona of Friedan's "happy housewife heroine," and Delk Adams, a Black woman, subverts that image in significant ways. Her recoding of the housewife and her food writing remembers food work of past generations, deconstructs the image of the stereotypical housewife as portrayed in popular culture, and challenges past stereotypical representations of Black women in the kitchen.

In her 8 March 2006 post "the best gluten free, dairy free, sugar free food you will ever eat," food blogger Shauna James Ahern (*Gluten-Free Girl*) writes of her visit to New York City's Lower East Side bakery Babycakes. The bakery, which is run by Erin McKenna, specializes in vegan goods and exudes a "kitschy, girly sensibility"— evocative of 1950s kitchen culture. Ahern reflects on what the bakery design—with its "nostalgic signs from the 1950s, talking about frosting shots and the inability to please everyone" means to her: "As an independent woman in 2006, I feel blessed that I have choices that my grandmother and mother never had. They were obligated to be in the kitchen, cooking away all day. But me? I choose it. I have that luxury. For me, the signs and sensibilities of Babycakes were a way of paying homage to that generation, winking at them as we bake." This "kitschy, girly sensibility" that Ahern observes upon visiting is evident on McKenna's website. The "Who Is Erin McKenna?" page reads, "In 2005, Erin McKenna's Bakery NYC opened on the Lower East Side of Manhattan with two rules: 1. Create a bakery free of harmful ingredients. 2. Wear cute uniforms." Foregrounded is the commitment to producing baked goods for "the underserved— people with gluten, dairy, egg, and soy sensitivities, the health-minded, and, most importantly, allergic kids who are often unable to indulge" ("Who Is Erin McKenna?"). Wearing cute uniforms (a wink, if you will) is second only to that mission. The images that appear on the website are in line with Ahern's characterization as well. There's lots of pink and purple and a heart over each letter "i." The images of the New York and Los Angeles locations show the outside of each storefront with a brightly painted door and what looks like homemade banners in the window; the image that accompanies the Orlando image shows the inside of the shop—painted pink. And McKenna herself appears in images on the website sporting bow-tied blouses and the shop's signature pink uniform complete with a Peter Pan collar.

Both Ahern's characterization of McKenna's bakery and McKenna's bakery itself deploy what Tony Fry, in his 2009 book

Design Futuring: Sustainability, Ethics, and New Practice, defines as recoding—"the transformation of the sign value of objects, images, structures, spaces, services and organizations" (81). Fry provides readers with a history of the term, connecting it to the study of the visual arts and noting how the technique "emerged out of modernist art practice during the nineteenth century" (81). Fry uses the art of Barbara Kruger as an example of this technique. Kruger, who is well known for her black-and-white photographs with overlaid text, often presents the viewer with a familiar image, yet the text that she overlays often changes their meaning for the viewer. As Christopher Bollen observes in *Interview*, "There is a distinctly Krugerian tone to all of her pieces . . . that compels the viewer to side with her and against her simultaneously, and always stop as the balance of our thinking shifts." For instance, *I Shop Therefore I Am* (1990) is an image of a black-and-white hand holding what looks like a red credit card. On the credit card are the words, "I Shop Therefore I Am," a phrase that invites viewers to interrogate their consumption practices ("Barbara Kruger"). In a more contemporary piece, *Untitled (Connect)* (2015), Kruger displays a smart phone home screen with the familiar square images that signify various apps. On those apps, however, are words such as "struggle," "fear," "envy," "rage," and "greed" ("Barbara Kruger: *Untitled (Connect)*"). Similarly, McKenna takes the traditional image of Friedan's "happy housewife heroine" and troubles it, and Ahern, in writing about her experience at the bakery, does so as well. Her description calls to mind Elizabeth Groeneveld's quote from *Making Feminist Media: Third-Wave Magazines on the Cusp of the Digital Age* (2016): "a campy performance of, and ironic commentary upon, a fictionalized domestic womanhood" (126).

Contemporary feminist publications, particularly the third wave feminist publications *Bitch* and *BUST*, often use recoding as a strategy in both their textual and visual discourse. *Bitch* and *BUST* are known for their witty takes on feminist issues. *BUST* describes itself as "a *cheeky* [my emphasis] celebration of all things female and a trusted authority on up-and-coming trends among discerning, educated, and culturally aware women" ("About *BUST*"). *Bitch* is equally sassy. Authors of its reoccurring column "Open Letter" often writes sarcastically regarding some current event, and the "Love It/ Shove It" column humorously debates the value of such current trends as the roles of heroines (Winter 2004) and representations of Islamic dress in cartoons (Winter 2005). Both publications' titles play with words. *Bitch* re-appropriates its name, and *BUST*'s slogan invokes its title: "For women with something to get off their chest." Visual recoding is key to these publications as well. On the Spring 2004 cover of *BUST*, comedic actress Tina Fey is clad in a tight, sexy black dress, making a surprised face. She's seated at a typewriter, and the accompanying text says, "Tina Fey: Geek Chic." Visually, the image invokes the suggestive covers of a men's magazine, but the text transforms the meaning of that image, emphasizing intelligence in addition to beauty.

Bitch often contains "kitschy" advertisements—some of which directly allude to the housewife of the Cold War Era. The advertisements for Repodepotfabrics.com of Burien, Washington and Psyche Therapy in Oakland, California, included in the publication, utilize old-fashioned imagery in ironic ways. Reprodepotfabrics.com, known for "retro textiles, clothing, and gifts," includes an illustration of 1950s-styled women enjoying a sewing circle. However, below the image, the advertised items, "vintage-looking fabrics," "cute cardigans," as well as "saucy lingerie," all update the image. Psyche boldly declares, "Not your mother's therapist," and includes a photograph of a 1950s woman, complete with a flipped-out bob hairstyle. Again, the visual and text both work to contradict each other, signaling to the reader that, while the image is recognizable, it will not be what you find at Psyche.

Elizabeth Groeneveld's *Making Feminist Media* presents readers with an assessment of third wave feminist rhetoric in popular feminist publications such as *BUST* and *Bitch*; Groeneveld historicizes the roles these publications have played in women's lives from the magazines' inceptions in the 1990s until today.[2] Her book includes chapters on the economics of these magazines as well as their reporting on such topics as fashion and sexuality. Groeneveld's chapter, "'Join the Knitting Revolution': Representations of Crafting in Feminist Magazines," most directly relates to this study. Here, Groeneveld examines the way in which these magazines reimagined—or recoded—domestic arts, particularly knitting. It's not surprising, Groeneveld reasons, that these magazines would include such content since zine culture largely inspired these commercial publications. 'Zine culture, she notes, has strong DIY principles and was central to the third wave feminist movement. But she also details the way in which these publications "update" the DIY movement, often including discourse that clearly differentiates the knitting practices of the present with the knitting practices of the past.[3]

Groeneveld expands upon this concept of the "neo-craft" in a section of this chapter titled "'Not Just for Grannies': The Generational Discourse of Neo-Craft." Groeneveld notes the ways in which feminist publications such as *BUST* and *Bitch* were embracing crafting but also distancing themselves from the crafting of earlier generation—hence the label "neo-craft." She writes:

> One of the most consistent aspects of craft discourse that appears in both feminist magazines and mainstream news media is the figuring of crafting hobbies as "new." Although there has been an intensification of crafting in recent years, what is at stake in continually figuring crafting practices in this way? This discourse allows media texts to self-construct as cutting edge and trend setting, a journalistic craft tradition that Patricia Bradley (2003) dubs "the lure of the new" (91). (122)

This strategy is at work in the title of popular writer Emily Matchar's 2013 book *Homeward Bound: Why Women Are Embracing the* New *Domesticity* (my emphasis). In her book, Matchar declares "the career girl—gone—Green Acres memoir is the new chick lit" (1).

As she explains in her 2011 opinion piece for the *Washington Post*, new domesticity is "a fantasy for a certain demographic of educated (though not necessarily wealthy) young women; today they're concerned with sustainability, good food and conscious living." In this article, Matchar lists what she calls "hipster home-ec books" that were recently published, and she interviews people such as Megan Paska, an urban gardener from Brooklyn, and Debbie Stoller, cofounder of *BUST* magazine, who wrote *Stitch and Bitch: The Knitter's Handbook* (2004); both women acknowledge the recent trend in finding value in domestic arts that were previously disparaged. For her book, Matchar interviewed young, educated, middle-class, white US American women who have returned to the domestic arts, and she looked at the way in which memoirs, fashion, food culture, and parenting represent a shift in twenty-first-century thinking about the domestic sphere.[4] Matchar is careful to note that while women might be practicing the domestic acts of their mothers and grandmothers, these acts are not the same; they are "new," distinct from those practiced in earlier eras.

The cover illustration of Matchar's book also presents readers with a clear, visual example of the process of third wave feminist recoding, particularly in regard to homemaking. On the book jacket is the illustration of a white woman knitting. She is surrounded by balls of yarn and a crock of cooking utensils. However, certain details recode this woman from a "happy housewife heroine," in Friedan's terms, to a hipster homemaker. She's wearing cat-eye glasses; there is a stripe of color in the front of her pixie-styled hair; and there is a tattoo peeking out of her sweater on her top, left-hand shoulder. While the image is familiar, it is also unfamiliar—an updated image of a common representation of white, middle-class US American women.

Groeneveld worries that "one effect of this persistent discourse of newness is that it also results in a distancing from the history of craft practices, eliding the important alliances—familial, political, aesthetic, and cultural—that might be forged in making these

Recoding Kitchen Space in Contemporary Food Writing   57

historical continuities more visible" (122). Her statement brings to mind the divisions between the second wave and third wave feminist movements. A common critique from second wave feminists is that third wave feminist discourse does not acknowledge the significant historical challenges, such as equal pay for equal work or the fight for reproductive rights, faced by the second wave generation. Like these contemporary crafters, food writers often deploy the label of "new," but, I would argue, they also resist this "distancing" from history by directly connecting their food work to the food work of previous generations. Food writers often update the image of the housewife, as McKenna does, thus recoding the space of the kitchen. But they also often simultaneously and deliberately acknowledge a past, as Ahern does in her blog post. Their work, then, is "actually in conversation with . . . an imagined"—and, I would also argue, real—"feminist past" (Groeneveld 117).

Food blogger and cookbook author Jocelyn Delk Adams, like McKenna and Ahern, acknowledges the food work of past generations. Delk Adams's cookbook *Grandbaby Cakes: Modern Recipes, Vintage Charm, Soulful Memories* contains not only recipes but stories and photographs of her family. She begins her introduction by noting, "You can't know where you are going until you know where you've been" (11). The introduction sets out to "honor" her ancestors—Black women—"who unknowingly shaped me into the fearless, confident, loving, driven woman I am through the decades of lessons learned in the kitchen" (14). The endpapers of her cookbook consist of various cooking gadgets with handwritten recipes strewn about the center. In her introduction, Delk Adams recalls how her family, who lived in Chicago while she was growing up, would frequently travel to Winona, Mississippi, where they would spend time visiting her mother's family. The women of her family would spend most of their time, she explains, in her grandmother's kitchen. It is fitting then that, while Delk Adams is the first photograph of a person in her cookbook, it is only three pages later that there is a photograph of Delk Adams's maternal grandmother, her mother, and her aunt. Delk Adams continues to honor these Black women throughout her book. At the start of each themed section, at least one of these four women is featured. Recipes credited to the women of her family—"Mama's 7UP Pound Cake" (31), "Aunt Irene's Apricot Nectar Cake" (50), and "Nana Pudding Tiramisu Cake" (103)—follow these photographs. In many of the recipes that are not directly credited to a family member, Delk Adams still references them. In her recipe for "Kentucky Brown-Butter Cake" (46), she shares a story of her Great-Aunt Henrietta in the preface to the recipe. In her recipe for "Snicker Cake" (173), Delk Adams writes of her daddy—a dentist who tried his best to curb her sweet tooth.

The title of Delk Adams cookbook belies one of the key themes of all her texts—"modern recipes, vintage charm." While she consistently draws attention to the food work of past generations, she also reminds readers of her "grandbaby" twist—or the way that she updates the cooking of the past for present generations. On her "About Me" page on her blog, she writes, "Welcome to Grandbaby Cakes, a brand inspired by my grandmother that shares classic recipes in a *modern* [my emphasis] and accessible way. I hope to inspire a *new* [my emphasis] generation of bakers and cooking enthusiasts to learn kitchen skills and not feel guilty about enjoying dessert." Delk Adams came to baking in her twenties, she explains, but embraced her "baking gene" in her thirties. She finishes off her "About Me" section by writing, "I achieve my ideal state of zen in my condo's cozy kitchen. . . . I remix traditional recipes with my fun 'grandbaby' twist." This "grandbaby twist" is a consistent theme throughout Delk Adams's website. In a section titled "I Got It from My Grandma," she invites readers to submit a favorite family recipe to be featured on her blog. She writes that she wants "to build a community of love and traditions that we can pass down and through our community," but she also notes that the recipes that will be selected and featured each month should "provide a new modern twist." Her site is peppered with contemporary references, which work to update this housewife image for the present. The title section, too, reminds readers of their place in the present. "I Got It from My Grandma" is a reference to the 2007 hip-hop song "I Got It from My Mama" by will.i.am. The merchandise Delk Adams sells also puts a hip, contemporary twist on the art of baking; she writes, "It's time to bring some fun back into the kitchen and the streets." She has a T-shirt that reads "DOPE" with the "o" being a donut. And there is another T-shirt that features the saying "Watch Me Whip/Watch Me Bake Cake," a reference to Silentó's 2015 hip-hop hit "Watch Me (Whip/Nae Nae)." In these moments, Delk Adams is not privileging the new over the old; rather, she resists "the lure of the new" that troubles Groeneveld in her analysis of contemporary crafters. Instead, she draws strong connections between the present and past rather than erasing that past.

A key component of Delk Adams's recoding of her kitchen space is her performance of Betty Friedan's "the happy housewife heroine." In *The Feminist Mystique*, Friedan describes the image of the housewife portrayed in women's magazines as such: "The image of woman that emerges from this big, pretty magazine [*McCall's*] is young and frivolous, almost childlike; fluffy and feminine; passive; gaily content in the world of bedroom and kitchen, sex, babies, and home" (82–83). The housewives in these magazines were often costumed in A-line skirts and frilly aprons. Their hair was coifed, and their makeup was impeccable; more often than not, they sported a bold, red lip. Like these housewives, Delk Adams is frequently dressed in colorful, flowery A-line dresses. The style is part of her branding; she is frequently seen in this old-fashioned attire in photographs for interviews or on television appearances. In a Q&A with *Room and Board*, she is featured in a pale peach frock with a string of pearls around her neck ("Q&A With Jocelyn Delk Adams of Grandbaby Cakes"). In a visit to the Food Network's *The Kitchen*, she sported an A-line navy blue and white gingham dress. Delk Adams's performance of the 1950s housewife "winks" (to call to mind Ahern's term) at the past while updating for the present.

Delk Adams's performance of the happy housewife heroine is similar to Erin McKenna's in that it is a "campy" performance of the housewife. But as a Black woman this performance is even more powerful. In recoding the traditional 1950s housewife as Black, Delk Adams not only critiques the image that most US Americans associate with the 1950s housewife, but she also reminds her US American audience of the stereotypical ways in which Black women in the kitchen have been presented in popular culture. As Friedan's work shows, but does not explicitly state, central to the identity of the happy housewife heroine is her race. While Friedan does not acknowledge that the target demographic for magazine publications she examines is white, in looking through past editions of the magazines, it becomes apparent that publications such as *McCall's* and *Good Housekeeping* consistently portrayed the "average" US American housewife as a white woman. Advertisements for products such as soap, face powder, hair coloring, and even tampons all portrayed smiling white women. While Friedan, in turn, does not explicitly state that *The Feminine Mystique* is about the white US American housewife, she is, in fact, writing about that demographic. And, as history has shown, the second wave feminist movement has been criticized for the way in which it privileged the issues of white women over those of women of color. In her self-fashioning as a "happy housewife heroine," I would argue that Delk Adams calls to mind the racial inequities associated with this time period in US American history.

As a Black woman, Delk Adams not only shifts the traditional image of Betty Friedan's "happy housewife heroine," creating for readers "a campy performance of, and ironic commentary upon, a fictionalized version of domestic womanhood" (Groeneveld 126), but she also comments upon past representations of Black women in the kitchen in US American popular culture. As Alice A. Deck begins in her essay "Now Then—Who Said Biscuits? The Black Woman Cook as Fetish in American Advertising, 1905–1953," "One of the prevailing images of Black women in American culture that has persisted since the early days of slavery is that of the quintessential cook and housekeeper" (69). Deck continues, describing this "mammy" figure as one who is physically imposing, masculine in stature but with feminine curves; she is an expert at not only cooking but delivering advice. Deck's essay outlines the ways in which US American advertisers capitalized on this image to sell products such as flour and pancake mix to white, female consumers. M. M. Manring explores a similar theme in *Slave in a Box: The Strange Career of Aunt Jemima* (1998). Manring, too, discussed the figure of the mammy, historicizing the way in which Aunt Jemima, as an advertising icon, developed out of that racist imagery. Manring argues, "From her beginnings in southern plantation reality and literature, the mammy was a sexual and racial symbol that was used by men and women, North and South, white and black to explain proper gender relationships, justify or condemn racial oppression, and establish class identities (for both whites and blacks)" (9).

Both Deck and Manring emphasize that an underlying message of these racist advertisements is the maintenance of racial social order. Some of these advertisements, they explain, feature a white woman, and the text of the advertisement makes it clear to the consumer that the mammy figure is there to serve in a supporting role to the white woman. Even in the advertisements that feature only the mammy figure, the subtext is, again, that the mammy is there to share her cooking secrets with the white female consumer. As Deck explains, "The fetishization of the black cook in American advertising for cooking and baking products reinforced the social position of white middle-class America as higher than that of black people, because it conveyed the idea that the black woman as the superior cook was actually a labor-saving device for whites" (80). Manring takes this reading a step further, noting that this depiction of Blacks in service to whites preserves "the power of the South—particularly, the plantation South"; the white consumer recognizes in these images "white leisure, abundance, and sexual order" (11).

Delk Adams's persona, then, counters these past representations in significant ways. Primarily, I would argue, Delk Adams puts herself and other Black women at the center of her narrative and at the center of her visuals that accompany her narrative. As noted earlier, in her cookbook and on her blog, she highlights the food work of past generations. She not only includes recipes from family, but she also includes photographs of these influential women. In 2021, Delk Adams was featured on the Food Network's *Around My Table*. The series, sponsored by Classico, features short webisodes where Delk Adams shares recipes with viewers using Classico products. In one episode, "Jocelyn and Joyce," Delk Adams cooks spaghetti and meatballs with her mother. While cooking, she discusses the influence that her mother and grandmother had on her personally and professionally. In another episode, "Jocelyn and Meiko," Delk Adams is joined by another Black food blogger, Meiko Temple (*Meiko and the Dish*). This spot begins with Delk Adams declaring, "Collard greens are vegetable gold in the black community." She notes, "I am in the kitchen with one of my fav boos, Meiko," before the two cook up a batch of collard-green-stuffed shells. While they cook, they talk about how Black culture has shaped their cooking styles, and they discuss how important it is for Black women to support one another, especially in the food industry. While Black women have long been relegated to the sidelines—from Aunt Jemima to such stereotypical film roles as the "sassy best friend" in romantic comedies—Delk Adams places herself and other Black women at the center of the narrative. She has countered those negative images with positive, joyful portrayals of Black women in the kitchen.

From her blog, Delk Adams was able to forget a professional career. Not only has she produced her blog and cookbook and served as a brand ambassador for such products as Classico, but she is also regularly featured on television programs such as *The Rachael Ray Show*, the Food Network's *The Kitchen*, and *Dr. Oz* and in magazines such as *O Magazine, Better Homes and Gardens*, and *Bon Appétit*. Before launching her blog, Delk Adams worked in licensing at *Ebony* magazine. Her colleagues encouraged her to start a baking blog after sampling the delicious homemade creations she brought into the office for her co-workers' birthdays (Wida). Many of those cakes were based on the creations of the women in her family. In her work, Delk Adams lifts up not only her own food work but also the food work of past generations of Black women, and in doing so, she rewrites the racist depictions of Black women in the space of the kitchen.

In the age of Black Lives Matter, Delk Adams presents readers and viewers with a powerful reminder of the ways in which the food world has been affected and continues to be affected by issues of inequality—from a tipping culture in the restaurant industry that emboldens patrons' sexual harassment to the prevalence of food deserts in areas occupied by low-income and racial minorities. This elitism, sexism, and racism is also apparent in celebrity food culture as explored by Josée Johnston and Shyon Baumann in *Foodies: Democracy and Distinction in the Gourmet Foodscape* (2010). Johnston and Baumann interrogate the socioeconomic history of food culture, noting the disparities that exist between the haves and the have-nots when it comes to food choices. When *Time* magazine ran a cover story in November 2013 titled "The 13 Gods of Food," only four women—none of whom were chefs—were featured (Chua-Eoan); a media uproar followed.[5] That same year, US Americans saw Food Network star and Southern restaurateur Paula Deen embroiled with scandal when she was caught using racial slurs. Most recently, cookbook author and former senior food editor at *Bon Appétit* Alison Roman found herself under fire after criticizing fellow cookbook author Chrissy Teigen and organization guru Marie Kondo for "selling out." As Lena Felton writes for *The Lily*, "[M]any followers have continued pointing out the nuances of this one: that a successful white woman was disparaging two successful Asian women, who are already a rarity in the food and lifestyle worlds."

Some might argue that the publishing world has done a better job than most in terms of inclusion. After all, writers such as Madhur Jaffrey, Diana Abu-Jaber, Cecilia Chiang, and Carla Hall have had successful careers. However, there are still particular voices being elevated and other voices being suppressed. Julia Turshen, author of *Feed the Resistance: Recipes and Ideas for Getting Involved* (2017), commented on this issue in an article for *Eater*, where she examines the racial bias in the cookbook niche of the food-writing world. She writes, "While cookbook publishing is often seen as a safe haven for women, as we occupy so much space in it, cookbook authors, agents, editors, publicists, food and prop stylists, photographers, book designers, and publishers are exceedingly white." Likewise, Kimberly Nettles-Barcelón points out in "Women and Entrepreneurial Food-Work" the continued homogeneity of race in what she calls "second act" food memoirs: memoirs in which writers exchange one job for another job in the food industry. Julie Powell's work falls into this genre as does the work of Molly Wizenberg and Gesine Bullock-Prado (*My Life from Scratch*, 2009). Nettles-Barcelón also points out the lack of economic diversity in food writing; she argues that writers of second act memoirs are often economically advantaged in some way, having both time and money to devote to their writing.

Finally, while the internet is said to have leveled the publishing playing field and there are, in fact, many excellent writers of color online today, many of the earliest food bloggers, the ones who received the most publicity, were white women. Writers such as Deb Perelman (*Smitten Kitchen*), Julie Powell (*The Julie/Julia Project*), Shauna James Ahern (*Gluten-Free Girl*), Molly Wizenberg (*Orangette*), and Ree Drummond (*The Pioneer Woman*) all received publishing contracts for cookbooks or memoirs. In looking over *The Guardian*'s "The 20 Best Food Books from 2001–2017," there is one book written by a husband-and-wife duo, nine books by women, and ten books by men. Of the nine women authors, three are women of color (Claudia Roden, born and raised in Egypt, spending much of her adult life in England; Meera Sodha, born and raised in England to Ugandan Asian parents; and Samin Nosrat, born and raised in America to Iranian immigrants); yet, none of those women are Black US Americans. Even more recently, when the *New York Times* published "The 14 Best Cookbooks of Fall 2020," racial inclusion was limited. Of the ten women listed, only one, Hawa Hassan, would be considered Black by US American definitions.[6] Delk Adams's presence in the online world and her subsequent success will hopefully inspire new generations of bloggers among women of color.

In 2013, Kerry Diamond and Claudia Wu founded *Cherry Bombe* magazine, a publication to celebrate women in food.[7] Each issue of the slick biannual magazine features articles on professionals in the food world, from chefs such as Gabrielle Hamilton to food stylists such as Victoria Granof to food scientists such as Lisa J. Mauer.[8] There are features on food-themed clothing and a recurrent column titled "Last Call," where celebrities such as Sofia Coppola and Chloe Sevigny share their favorite cocktails.

Diamond and Wu's publication is remarkable for several reasons. To start, the magazine includes diverse content, highlighting all different aspects of the food world. In the inaugural issue, which featured supermodel and cookie entrepreneur Karlie Kloss on the cover, there was an article on the seed vault (also known at the Doomsday Vault) in Norway, a fruit-inspired hat by designer Piers Atkinson, Camas Davis's (Portland Meat Collective, a butchery and charcuterie school) meditations on good knives, and an interview with Harvard microbiologist Rachel Dutton. The magazine also includes food-inspired writings from personal memoirs to interviews with celebrated greats such as Alice Waters and Judith Jones. Rather than distancing themselves from their past, *Cherry Bombe* intentionally highlights the work of established women in the food world. *Cherry Bombe* has included established food celebrities, such as Ruth Reichl (spring/summer 2014) and Martha Stewart (spring/summer 2017), as well as up-and-coming food celebrities, such as Erin McKenna (fall/winter 2013) and Kristen Kish (fall/winter 2014) on their covers. Most importantly, perhaps, the publication is committed to featuring women who occupy a variety of subject positions—particularly in terms of race and sexuality. Issue 15 (spring/summer 2020) features Paola Velez, cofounder of Bakers against Racism, whose global bake sale made almost $2 million for local

Black Lives Matter causes. This issue also highlights the work of the Okra Project, "a collective that seeks to address the global crisis faced by Black Trans people by bringing home cooked, healthy, and culturally specific meals and resources to Black Trans People" (The Okra Project), and Heart of Dinner, an organization dedicated to "ending hunger and isolation for low-income Asian-American homebound elderly" people. They "source, cook, and deliver culturally appropriate meals" (Heart of Dinner).

In the spring/summer 2017 issue, which features Martha Stewart on the cover, Julia Turshen interviewed a variety of food professionals for a piece titled "Activism Is the New Normal." Delk Adams is one of the people featured. She speaks to the issues of racial inequality in the food world:

> As a brand, my activism is tied to creating a space for someone who looks like me and shares my cultural ties to escalate to greater heights in my industry. Sure there are a few success stories sprinkled here and there. Carla Hall and Sunny Anderson come to mind. But until I see a black woman ascend to the heights of Martha Stewart, Ina Garten, or Rachael Ray, I will keep fighting for that spot or helping others who come after me fight for it. (90)

Delk Adams's presence in the food world and her active support of women of color in the industry reveals the many ways in which food and the preparation of it are both a powerful and political act.

4

KITCHEN SPACES

Sites of Resistance and Transformation

In the very first episode of *Nigella Bites* (2001), which was broadcast in the United States on both E! and the Style Network, cookbook author and soon to be television personality Nigella Lawson declares, "What I'm after is minimum effort for maximum pleasure in both the cooking and the eating."[1] From an armchair in her home, she confides to the viewer, "The idea here, for me, is food that I love eating but doesn't give me a nervous breakdown to cook."[2] Throughout that first season, we see Lawson dip a piece of beef into béarnaise sauce and eat it with her fingers ("Family") and prepare and eat what she labels "cheese flavored chewing gum" (mozzarella in carrozza) for the way in which she eats it—in long strands, dripping straight into her mouth ("TV Dinners").

By the time *Nigella Bites* aired, Nigella Lawson had already established herself as a writer, a cook, and, to some, a celebrity. Besha Rodell, in an article for the *New York Times*, quotes British food writer Diana Henry, who describes Lawson as such: "In the U.K. I often think—not with pleasure—that she has Princess Diana-like status as a celebrity. She is that well known, she is that well liked."[3]

Prior to filming the series, Lawson had a successful career as a journalist, writing for such diverse publications as the *Daily Telegraph*, *Vogue*, and *Gourmet*. Her first book, *How to Eat: The Pleasures and Principles of Good Food* (1998) was heralded for its "narrative form . . . the recipes told like stories." In fact, the focus is so much on the narrative that there are no photographs of the finished dishes; rather, there are artful photographs throughout of such items as kitchen utensils and vegetables. She followed the success of *How to Eat* with her second cookbook, *How to Be a Domestic Goddess: Baking and the Art of Comfort Cooking* (2000).

Cultural critics and scholars have made note of the way in which Lawson has impacted food culture—particularly in regard to women's enjoyment of the food they have cooked and the acknowledgment that women do, indeed, have appetites. In "Feeling Like a Domestic Goddess: Postfeminism and Cooking," cultural critic Joanne Hollows observes, "[Lawson's] cooking style is carefully distanced from the prim and proper efficiency of the (female) home economist and the decontextualized precision of the (male) professional chef" (182). As Lynn Hirschberg remarks in writing for the *New York Times Magazine*, most of the episodes in Lawson's series include Lawson licking her fingers or "test[ing] a dish by tilting her head way back and dangling a noodle or string bean into her open mouth," thoroughly enjoying something she had just cooked up. As Bee Wilson writes for *The Guardian* in 2018, "[Lawsons'] voice [was one] of a woman who did not feel the need to hide or disguise her own appetites, as so many of us are taught to do." For these writers, Lawson's body of work has become a transgressive force in the world of cooking and eating, which frequently encouraged women's preparation but not enjoyment of food.

Despite Lawson's progressive messaging about women's appetites, or maybe because of it, the press has often preoccupied themselves with Lawson's personal appearance. Writers often manage to work some sort of surveillance of Lawson's body into their pieces.

Kitchen Spaces: Sites of Resistance and Transformation   69

For instance, Hirschberg writes, "[E]verything about [Lawson] looks ripe, from her brown eyes to her full lip, to her breasts, which are accentuated by tight sweaters." Writing about an episode in which Lawson makes fresh guacamole, *The Guardian*'s Jacques Peretti recounts, "'Oh, that's just how I like it,' she says, smoothing her Morticia hair and pouting—oh cruel and terrible beauty—into the camera." *Belfast News Letters*' Patrick Ryans describes the television personality: "Good-looking and raven-haired, her features are Mediterranean, her body generously endowed and her eyes dark as midnight." Before long, the press began dubbing her "yummy mummy." While Lawson celebrated her love of food in her cookbooks and on television, the press focused on her outward appearance, often reducing her to nothing more than the object of the male gaze.[4]

This media's preoccupation with Lawson's body is not something unique to Lawson. Actresses who gain weight or who are deemed "too skinny" are often criticized in the press. The food world is no exception. Fans have created sites dedicated to the "Top 10 Female Chefs," "The Eight Sexiest Women on Cooking Shows," and "The Hottest Women of the Food Network." The popular press loves to comment on celebrity chef Giada De Laurentiis's appearance from her "low-cut T-shirt[s]" to her "tiny frame."[5] When searching *Top Chef* judge Padma Lakshmi, numerous websites promising "hot shots" come up. Conversely, when a female food celebrity gains weight, the press is sure to notice. In February 2017, *Radar Online* published the article, "Rachael Ray's Job In Jeopardy Over Massive Weight Gain?: The food Guru is eating herself out of a career!" (Gamez). Cooking columnist for *The Sun*, Lorraine Pascale goes so far as to ask, "Why are people obsessed with the size of female chefs? No one ever calls Gordon Ramsay fat" (Jackson). Pascale points to a very real double standard when it comes to men and women. As feminist scholars have noted, women's bodies—in the food world and beyond—have long been subject to surveillance.

In this chapter, I look at two food memoirs that serve as a site of resistance to the negative messaging that women often receive about the preparation and consumption of food—Giulia Melucci's *I Loved, I Lost, I Made Spaghetti: A Memoir of Good Food and Bad Boyfriends* (2010) and Kim Sunée's *Trail of Crumbs: Hunger, Love, and the Search for Home* (2009). These memoirs challenge assumptions about women's appetites, particularly their relationships with the food that they prepare and eat. The home kitchen becomes a vital space to these authors' growth and development. Melucci must unlearn that the idea that cooking will secure her a husband; Sunée must reclaim the home kitchen in order to heal herself from an unhealthy relationship. Melucci's and Sunée's memoirs, I argue, serve as a site of resistance, an "emancipatory counter-discourse" (Lazar qtd. in Jovanovski 31); the preparation of food and the enjoyment of it are a vital component to these women writers' growth and development.

Women's appetites have long been a topic of feminist scholars.[6] Tamar Heller and Patricia Moran in their introduction to *Scenes of the Apple: Food and the Female Body in Nineteenth- and Twentieth-Century Women's Writing* trace this preoccupation as far back as the biblical story of a "hungry Eve" (2). In their introduction, they contextualize this preoccupation, noting that a major contributor to the control of women's appetites was, and still is, the fashion industry. The authors observe that, at the turn of the century, "not only did the hourglass figure give way to the ideal of a boyish, prepubescent outline, but the new affordability and access to ready-made clothing—as opposed to making one's clothing or having it sewn by a dressmaker—meant that middle-class women had to adapt themselves to standard or normal shapes in order to be fashionable" (11). Scholars such as Susan Bordo (*Unbearable Weight*, 1993) and Jean Kilbourne (*Can't Buy My Love*, 1999) have eloquently argued that the media presents women with harmful messages about their appetites—not only in terms of eating but also in terms of sexuality.[7]

Natalie Jovanovski's recent book *Digesting Femininities: The Feminist Politics of Contemporary Food Culture* (2017) is the

Kitchen Spaces: Sites of Resistance and Transformation 71

scholarship most germane to *Season to Taste*. Jovanovski's discussion of the surveillance of women's bodies in contemporary culture acknowledges, like her scholarly predecessors, the connections between media images and women's body policing. While Jovanovski understands the importance of the scholarship that has proceeded her, she argues that much of this scholarship has been "body-centric, focusing on how the size and shape of the female body is depicted in the media and overlooking the power of other significant discourses in perpetuating self-objectifying messages" (2). Instead, Jovanovski's book examines food discourse, such as that in weight loss books, cookbooks, and even feminist theory, arguing that these mediums present women with just as powerful—and damaging—messages about their relationship with food. More specifically, Jovanovski explores how female celebrity chefs (un)consciously deploy these food femininities in her chapter "Cooking Up Femininities: Motherhood, Hedonism and Body-Policing in Popular Cookbooks." She writes:

> In this chapter, I examine how the uncomfortable intersection of gender and food is reinforced by female celebrity cooks in mainstream, best-selling cookbooks. I also explore how the advice given to female audiences rests upon a narrative of both traditional and contemporary food femininities. It is the tension between the maternal (i.e., the traditional feeder) and the hedonistic (i.e., the contemporary eater) where body-policing narratives are expressed, an indication that the male gaze operates to colonize both women's ability to feed others and themselves. (105)

In her discussion of such celebrity chefs as Tara Ramsey, Julie Goodwin, Poh Ling Yeow, and even Nigella Lawson, Jovanovski reveals the anxieties and tensions in their cookbooks. She argues that some of these cookbooks, like those of Ramsey's, reinforce the performance of "good" motherhood through food preparation and that others, like Lawson's, ultimately fall prey to the body policing necessitated by male surveillance despite attempts to shift the focus to an enjoyment of food and eating.[8]

A genre that Jovanovski does not examine is that of women's food writing, particularly the trend of memoirs with recipes that surged in the first two decades of the twenty-first century. As I noted in my introduction, both Melucci's and Sunée's books were published as the popular fiction phenomenon known as chick lit was waning. Melucci and Sunée are, like the heroines of this genre (Bridget Jones from Helen Fielding's *Bridget Jones's Diary*, 1996, and Carrie Bradshaw from Candace Bushnell's *Sex and the City*, 1996), young women living in metropolitan areas navigating their love relationships. Unlike chick lit, whose heroines were often presented as struggling with their consumption practices (eating, shopping, and sex, for example), food writing often resists the standard, negative messaging that US American women often receive about food, and the memoirs serve as a site of resistance; the kitchen becomes a space of transformation. For instance, in her introduction to *Spoon Fed* (2010), Kim Severson writes about the way in which she needed the kitchen to learn necessary life lessons; these lessons came from women who acted as her "guides" (7). "[T]heir kitchens were my classrooms," she writes (7). Many of these memoirs highlight a particular obstacle in the author's life, which the author can only "solve" by returning to the kitchen. In Julie Powell's best-selling memoir, *Julie & Julia* (2005), Powell writes about how her project—to cook every recipe in Julia Child's *Mastering the Art of French Cooking* in one year—enabled her to escape the drudgery of her administrative job.[9] Eventually, this project led her to a different career entirely. In the case of Molly Wizenberg (*Orangette*), blogging about food gave her an outlet while she was struggling as a graduate student enrolled in an anthropology PhD program.

The marketing for many of these books plays up this common theme. Very often, somewhere on the packaging of the book, the reader will find a summary that highlights the way in which the kitchen becomes a place of transformation for the authors. The

Kitchen Spaces: Sites of Resistance and Transformation 73

description on the back cover for the paperback edition of Gesine Bullock-Prado's *My Life from Scratch* (2009) highlights how Bullock-Prado's love of baking becomes the catalyst for her new life: "*My Life from Scratch* follows Gesine's journey from sugar-obsessed child to awkward Hollywood insider to burgeoning baker."[10] Similarly, on the inside flap of the hardcover edition of Kate Moses's *Cakewalk* (2010), the kitchen is described as "the one realm where [Moses] was able to wield control" amid her chaotic family life. The quotes included on the packaging of many of these books also focus on the theme of self-actualization and the role that the kitchen plays in that. A quote from Bookslut.com on the back of the paperback edition of Cathy Erway's *The Art of Eating In: How I Learned to Stop Spending and Love the Stove* (2010) reads, "Erway's journey is one of a young artist finding herself, as a cook, as a member of several interesting communities, as a family member, and as a writer." In describing Jackie Kai Ellis's *The Measure of My Powers: A Memoir of Food, Misery, and Paris* (2017), Jen Waite, author of *A Beautiful, Terrible Thing*, writes, "With searing vulnerability and unflinching honesty, Jackie Kai Ellis takes us on an intense and immersive journey from her darkest moments to the redemption she finds through her love of food, Paris, and, ultimately, herself."

Waite's description or Kai Ellis's book stresses an important aspect of many of these food memoirs with recipes: the authors' "love of food." While the preparation of the food is integral to these texts, these authors also share their love of eating with their readers. This holds true for books such as *The Art of Eating In*, where the emphasis on enjoying food is foregrounded in the title of the book, but it also holds true for books such as Kathleen Flinn's *The Sharper Your Knife, the Less You Cry* (2008), where ostensibly the emphasis is on the preparation, not the enjoyment, of food. At the forefront of Flinn's text is her recounting her cooking experiences as a student at Le Cordon Bleu, but she also chronicles moments of eating out in Paris, enjoying roasted quail, veal stew, or fondue. For other writers, such as blogger Shauna James Ahern (*Gluten-Free Girl*), food literally heals her body. On her blog, Ahern chronicles her struggle with celiac disease; she shares gluten-free recipes with readers that ease the pain of her disease and keep her from being symptomatic. Many of the authors mentioned here include recipes that accompany their narrative proper. These recipes serve as a further investment in the food that they have prepared, eaten, and enjoyed.

Giulia Melucci's memoir, *I Loved, I Lost, I Made Spaghetti* (2010) is one of these food memoirs in which the author needs the kitchen and cooking in order to heal. Melucci recounts her experiences as a young, single woman in New York City. Like her chick lit predecessors, she adopts a conversational tone as she shares some disastrous dating experiences with her readers. On one hand, Melucci embraces the role of the hedonist—satiating her appetite for both sex and food throughout the memoir. On the other hand, the strongest narrative thread of Melucci's text rests with her attempts to secure a husband by feeding her boyfriends well, a narrative thread that seems more in line with Jovanovski's critique of women as feeders. However, despite the prominent role that the preparation of food plays in Melucci's text, the resolution of her narrative ultimately undermines this messaging about women, their roles in the kitchen, and their relationships with food. At the conclusion of Melucci's text, she realizes that she cannot rely upon a man to make her happy; rather, she must create her own happiness.

At the onset of her text, Melucci articulates her approach to dating: "Whenever I start dating someone new, I just can't hold back. No matter how often my girlfriends warn me, 'Take it slow, let him win you over, don't give it away so quickly,' I just can't resist—I have to cook for him" (1). She continues, "For me, a new boyfriend is a tantalizing opportunity to show off the thing I am most confident about: my cooking" (1). This opening speaks to some of the tensions that Jovanovski writes of in *Digesting Femininities*—the traditional feeder/hedonist opposition. The inclusion of the phrase "give it away so quickly" sets up a misleading expectation for the reader who, at first, might think that Melucci is talking about sex when she is really

Kitchen Spaces: Sites of Resistance and Transformation 75

talking about preparing food. This quote by Melucci calls to mind Jovanovski's description of Nigella Lawson, who, Jovanovski argues, exhibits a "conflation of sexuality with the desire to eat" (117). Like Lawson, Melucci often blurs the line between her appetites, as shown above. Good meals and good sex go hand in hand for Melucci. Each relationship starts with some sort of meal—Kit ("Fried Eggplant" and "Simple Tomato Sauce and Pasta for Two"), Ethan ("Healthy Penne," "Unforgettable Halibut," and "Linguine with Friendly Little Fish"),[11] Mitch ("First-Date Butterflies"), Marcus ("Dinner to Impress an Older Gentleman: Grilled Marinated Flank Steak" and "Fried Red Potatoes"), and Lachlan ("Lachlan's Rigatoni with Eggplant"). And, throughout her memoir, Melucci shares the details of her sexual relationships with each man. In Melucci's memoir, sex, love, and food are inextricably linked.

Not only does Melucci prepare meals for her boyfriends to enjoy, but she takes pleasure in them as well. In fact, Melucci is frank about her need to satisfy her appetites—whether in the bedroom or in the kitchen. Melucci delights in sex. When she and Ethan finally sleep together, she writes, "'Unprecedented,' is how Ethan labeled what took place over the next four hours" (76). Melucci unabashedly shares with readers her skill in the bedroom and her enjoyment of sex. Melucci is equally zealous about a good meal. For instance, while dating Marcus, she takes him out to visit her family in Connecticut. While there, she makes "lamb burgers accompanied by slices of tomatoes from the farmer's market drizzled with olive oil and sprinkled with fleur de sel along with an orzo salad with feta cheese. We created old-fashioned strawberry shortcakes from the leftover biscuits, slicing them in half and layering them with strawberries and whipped cream" (162). Her descriptions, "drizzled with olive oil" and layered with fruit and cream, are ones of an eater, and in fact, she notes that she, Marcus, and her aunt "had a thoroughly enjoyable meal" (162). Very rarely do we see Melucci sitting by while a boyfriend eats her meal; instead, she fervently joins in. On occasion, Melucci will note that she was "plump," or after

76   Kitchen Spaces: Sites of Resistance and Transformation

a particularly good meal, she might remark on how "fat" she felt (28). While Melucci's narrative contains the occasional mention of her body in negative terms, more often than not, Melucci counteracts these body-policing moments with many more moments that celebrate her body through her enjoyment of both sex and food.

On the surface, Melucci's focus is on the preparation of food for others—her enjoyment of the role of traditional feeder. While she does enjoy the dishes she prepares, her main objective in cooking seems to be to ensnare a husband. Melucci's narrative includes stories about five major men in her life—Kit, Ethan, Mitch, Marcus, and Lachlan.[12] Each of these relationships is recounted through the meals that were prepared. For instance, in order to win over Kit, who prefers drinking to cooking, she makes her Nana's blueberry muffins and his mother's meatloaf. Her relationship with Ethan is largely successful at first because he enjoys her cooking. As with Kit, she appeals to Ethan's appetites, at one point preparing a Seder dinner for him to prove that she can be the Jewish wife he's always wanted. Mitch isn't particularly interested in food, but Melucci tries to win him over with grilled cheese, pasta with butter, and a meat and potatoes Valentine's Day dinner. He declares, "Everything associated with you is delicious" (126). Melucci explicitly states, when her relationship with Marcus goes offtrack, "The discomfort will go away if I try just a little harder or make something that tastes really, really good" (167). For Melucci, the way to a man's heart is through his stomach, and with her top-notch culinary skills, it follows that securing a husband should come easily. Melucci reasons at one point that God wouldn't "bless me with such well-honed domestic skills, then deny me a family to share them with" (182).

Yet none of these relationships work out. The last boyfriend that Melucci writes about in her memoir is Lachlan; he is the one that comes closest to committing to Melucci. His narrative is the one that Melucci devotes the most time, and recipes, to. He greatly appreciates her food, and Melucci goes to great lengths to strategically make meals that she hopes will win him over. When he indicates that he might return overseas, she makes him "Maryland Colony Crab Cakes," which she feels sure will keep him longing for the United States. When he returns from Italy, she makes him "Welcome Back to the Big Apple Muffins."

As noted above, Melucci is puzzled as to why she would be blessed with domestic skills if she couldn't share them with a husband. She writes, "I was in my late thirties, I wanted to have a real home with a real kitchen where my husband and I would host my brothers and sisters, nieces and nephews for holidays" (182). This investment in securing domestic bliss is one that preoccupies her throughout the narrative, and it is also one that often blinds her to her suitors' less desirable qualities. In Lachlan's case, it is both his disregard for Melucci's investment in his success and his lack of interest in sex that become the turning point for her relationship with him. Melucci, who works in the book business, sets out to secure him—a previously published novelist—both an agent and a book deal. However, the process is exceedingly stressful, and Melucci sees no appreciation on the part of Lachlan. She writes, "Lachlan's lack of concern for the needs of my body . . . was doing me in" (254). While in the moment Melucci is referencing the work that she is doing in procuring Lachlan an agent, her statement resonates in other ways. Melucci expresses concern for Lachlan's lack of interest in sex—something that she feels is paramount to a healthy relationship. Melucci invests quite a bit in Lachlan: she helps him with his career and makes him meals. While Melucci includes two of Lachlan's recipes in his section, the majority of the recipes are hers, which speaks to the incredible amount of time and effort she has put into becoming the traditional feeder. She cares for him in a variety of ways, yet she feels no reciprocation.

This preoccupation with preparing food for men shows how traditional gender roles influence Melucci's sense of self. Nearly every recipe in her book was made for a man that she was dating.[13] While this focus might give the impression that—like the food discourses that Jovanovski examines—*I Loved, I Lost, I Made*

Spaghetti simply reinforces traditional messaging about women as feeder, Melucci's narrative resolution undermines this supposition. Just prior to meeting Lachlan, Melucci decides to search for an apartment of her own in a chapter appropriately titled "Single Girl Suppers." She finds one that she falls in love with and sets about transforming it into her home. Lachlan moves in for a short while. This arrangement, however, does not live up to her expectations. Ultimately, she concludes that this space is better not shared. It seems fitting that when Melucci finally realizes that things will not work out for them, she shouts, "Just make us something for dinner!" Exhausted from feeding and caring for Lachlan, it is not long before their relationship completely disintegrates, and Melucci is left alone in her own kitchen space.

The closing of Melucci's narrative shows the progress she has made in ridding her kitchen of the specter of her future husband and learning to appreciate the kitchen as her own space. Immediately after Lachlan leaves, she begins writing her book—the one that chronicles her loves and losses. She explains how she imagines that book to begin:

> "What do you want to know?" it opened. "How much money he got for the book or how much he broke my heart?" I imagined an entire book about Lachlan, ending with the line "Reader, they overpaid."
>
> But then I thought, Why let him alone have all the glory? Even though that experience, the first to leave me feeling both heartbroken and used, certainly was the grated cheese atop the bowl of spaghetti. I wrote about all of them, and I kept on cooking. (269)

Melucci doesn't abandon the space of the kitchen; rather, she returns to it on her own terms, ending with the chapter "True Pasta Waits." Here, she confesses to never having made homemade pasta. It wasn't until she had a space of her own that she began to experiment with this act of cooking. She concludes this chapter with a final, simple recipe:

Kitchen Spaces: Sites of Resistance and Transformation 79

Homemade Pasta
  Flour
  Eggs
  I don't know the exact measure.
  I'm still trying to figure out the steps. (278)

In reading this final recipe, it becomes clear that the "made spaghetti" of Melucci's title does not refer to her feeding the men in her life (after all, she never tried to make pasta from scratch until this point in time). Rather, she is cooking for herself.

While Melucci confronts the specter of a future husband in her memoir, Kim Sunée must confront the physical presence of her partner, Olivier Baussan, in the kitchen space.[14] Throughout Sunée's memoir, Olivier uses food to assert control over Sunée. Early in their relationship, Olivier labels Sunée "mistress of the house" (xvii), and he expects her to prepare elaborate meals for all of his visiting guests. The kitchen, which was previously a place of peace for Sunée, becomes representative of her imprisonment within this relationship. The consumption of food and the space of the kitchen become a battleground, and Sunée finds herself fighting to (re)claim this space as a symbolic way to obtain some of the power that Olivier wields over her.

Throughout *Trail of Crumbs*, Sunée writes of feeling out of place, no matter what geographical region she inhabits; she strongly desires to locate a place that she can call home. The feeling of displacement that she felt as a child pervades her narrative. Sunée, who was born in Korea, was adopted and raised by a family from New Orleans, Louisiana. As a child, she looked different from her classmates; they mock her and her sister: "They even sing a little song and tug at their eyes until they're stretched like knife slits. 'Chinese, Japanese,' they taunt. 'Dirty knees, look at these'" (7). In a memory from this time, she recalls her adopted father noting that Asian people's muscle structure is different. She finds it difficult to assimilate to her adopted family's culture, and as soon as she has the chance, she leaves to go to school in Florida. When Sunée move to Provence with Olivier, she feels equally out of place. Sunée proves to be an object of fascination for Olivier's friends. She notes that their guests will wonder where she is from; she imagines them seeing her as just "an Asian face telling stories in French about *la Nouvelle-Orléans, le jazz, las cuisine Créole*" (xvii). While visiting Corsica, Olivier's friends and relatives observe that Sunée is a bit skinny (109). When she visits Korea with Olivier, she imagines people staring at her, and at an upscale restaurant she and Olivier are mocked because they assume Sunée is a prostitute—out to dinner with a white man. Unlike Melucci, who doesn't express anxiety about her cultural identity (she is of Italian descent and spends most of her time with upwardly mobile, white people throughout her book), Sunée, in her memoir, reflects upon her cultural heritage, noting how these observations about her Asian American, female body impact her sense of self, and she continually expresses a longing for a home where she feels at peace with her intersecting identities.

Olivier's relationship with Sunée seems largely informed by what cultural critics have labeled the docility myth—the idea that Asians, particularly women, are "exoticized and celebrated for docility" (Chou and Feagin 19).[15] When Sunée moves into Olivier's home, it becomes apparent that he is in charge of both the public and private realms of his life. Olivier is an extremely successful business, but on the very first page of her memoir, Sunée also emphasizes the power that Olivier commands in the domestic realm. As she sits outside, lounging by the pool, she notes, "I hear his voice every now and then as he goes from room to room" (xv). Though she has positioned herself outside of the home itself, she is still unable to escape Olivier. It's significant, too, that in this moment she hears him giving orders—this time to "the artisan from Carcassonne" who will repaint the house. Olivier controls his home, and he expects Sunée to follow his orders and live up to his expectations regarding obedience.

Throughout the memoir, Sunée portrays Olivier as a commanding figure; she comments that he is "always making sure everyone

Kitchen Spaces: Sites of Resistance and Transformation 81

knows his place, his unquestionable way of making the world turn in his direction" (85). And, as we see in the introduction, he is particularly controlling of Sunée—defining her role within his home. She explains that Olivier has made her "mistress of the house" (xvii), yet she does not ever feel entirely at home within that space. The few possessions that she does bring with her to Olivier's home are sequestered in "the office that Olivier has insisted [she] take as [hers]" (71). Olivier designates this space as Sunée's "writing room" (71), but while it is filled with her things, it is still not hers. Olivier decorates it with "a thick beechwood table" and "his father's cane-seat chair" (71) and conveniently locates it in a room that serves as "the only path from the inside of the house that leads to Olivier's wine cellar" (71). The implication is that Olivier, and others, are able to intrude at will.

Olivier's kitchen becomes a battleground between the couple, and it is in this space where the imbalance of power in their relationship is most noticeable. Throughout her narrative, Sunée acknowledges her skill in the kitchen. When she travels abroad to France for the first time as an undergraduate, her host mother teaches her to cook, and she explains in the chapter following, "I started to relish the subtle powers of knowing my way around a kitchen" (39). She shares stories of cooking "sweet pea salad with mint and bacon . . . omelet of wild asparagus dusted with fragrant thyme blossoms" for a group of male roommates in Nice, of cooking gumbo in Sweden for a man she thought loved her. The recipes that she includes in these early chapters show her skill in the kitchen as well—"Croque-Madame," "Chestnut-Mascarpone Rolls," and "Almond Saffron Cake." Though Sunée may express feeling like an outsider in all of the countries she travels to, she also reveals that the kitchen, in each of these places, is a constant; this is the space where she can locate a sense of self.

As a child, too, the kitchen was the space where Sunée and her adopted sister, Suzy, would spend time, particularly when they returned home from school, where they were constantly bullied by their classmates for their flat noses and being called names such as

"Genghis Khan," "Chink," and "Gook." Her childhood home kitchen was commandeered by her grandfather, Poppy. Sunée writes that "the comfort of Poppy's kitchen after school every day, the promise of his home-cooked meals, are a refuge, a safe place where our grandparents nourish us—solid food to remind us that we exist, that we live in a new world where we have not been forgotten" (11).

Olivier, however, does not approach his kitchen space like Poppy. Poppy eagerly invites his grandchildren to *share* in the kitchen space while Olivier relegates Sunée to his kitchen space, having determined that she is "suited" for it (xvii). Early in the narrative, Sunée notes that, while she may appear "fearless and without age" in Olivier's kitchen, his kitchen is not her own (xviii). Yet, Olivier determines that Sunée should prepare meals for the friends and family who pass through and stay with the couple throughout the summer. In "Where I Am," Sunée and Sophie, the wife of the property manager, visit the market to prepare for a meal, selecting "ripe melons," "the fattest white asparagus," and "the best salt-cured ham" (xvi–xvii). It is always Olivier who "roasts the meat and chooses the wine" (xvii), making his presence in the space known.

During these meal preparations, it is almost as though Sunée is Olivier's sous chef, not his romantic partner. Sunée prepares the fava bean salad, but Olivier tests the mint sauce. For one of the last meals of the summer, Sunée debates whether to prepare lamb or "roasted *cabri*" (120), but Olivier ultimately decides that rabbit is best. He may designate the space as Sunée's, but he uses every opportunity to encroach upon that space. Sunée's memories of "Olivier's kitchen" (63), then, are often ones in which she remembers feeling alienated, not quite at peace with herself. Any pleasant recollections of her time in the kitchen are often clouded by a memory of Olivier "circling the house" (63); though he is not physically present, he still makes his presence known. From the very first page, Sunée characterizes Olivier as the one in control over the home, even if she is deemed "the mistress of the house" (xvii).

In the chapter titled "The Monk's Table," we can clearly see the way in which his constant surveillance has taken its toll on her. Sunée begins this chapter with "Sometimes I need to remind myself where I am" (118)—an allusion back to her prelude. While Sunée follows this declaration with the recording in her notebook of actual places she has traveled, the words remind the reader of the central theme of this chapter and Sunée's memoir as a whole. In it, Sunée expresses to Olivier her desire for a role beyond that of "mistress" of his house, and she confides to the reader that she is "uncomfortable as the hostess" for Olivier's friends and family (119). When Olivier brings home a monk's table, which seats thirty, Sophie sees the implications, noting, "Thirty hungry mouths around that table. *Ma pauvre*, you've got some work ahead of you" (121). Olivier's decision to expand the seating capacity in their kitchen corresponds with Sunée's desire to seek some sort of fulfillment outside of the home. It is as though buying the larger table will further confine her to the space of the kitchen, planning, prepping, and preparing food for visitors.

While Sunée has willingly obeyed Olivier in the past, the monk's table prompts her first act of significant rebellion—a true turning point for Sunée's relationship with Olivier. At the first, and last, dinner at that table, the seats are filled, and there is talk of opening a bed and breakfast. Immediately following that scene, Sunée relates Olivier's decision for the two of them to visit Korea, Sunée's birthplace, a trip she has been reluctant to take. When the carpenters arrive about a week later to do work on the house, she asks one of them to cut off a third of the table, noting that cooking for thirty people each and every night is a huge burden. Her act is noteworthy. She defies Olivier's wishes and restructures the kitchen space according to her specifications—not his. With her doing so, we begin to see the first signs of her establishing her own identity outside of her relationship with Olivier, of figuring out who she is and where she wants to be without his help.

Likewise, in the chapters that follow "The Monk's Table," Sunée continues to slowly pull away from Olivier as he increases his control over her. One of the chief ways that Sunée realizes the degree to which her relationship with Olivier is unhealthy is through her changing relationship with food. During the most stressful moments of her relationship, Sunée expresses her distress by recalling her inability to cook and eat. When the two embark on a trip to Korea, China, and Hong Kong, the trip that Sunée did not want to take but that Olivier arranged regardless, Sunée becomes physically ill. The entire chapter, "With Reservations," is uncomfortable, filled with Sunée's recollections of her illness and horrifying memories of heat, noise, people devouring fish whole, furry thousand-year-old eggs, children playing in garbage.[16] The last image imprinted in Sunée's mind from the trip is as follows: "[A] man squatting at the edge of the water. . . . He slices open the throat of a turtle, rocks back and forth as if humming a lullaby. I watch him watch it bleed to death" (178). This chapter marks a significant moment in Sunée's journey. As in "The Monk's Table," Sunée realizes here that food and the space of the kitchen have become tainted by Olivier's constant demands and controlling attitude; she recognizes that she must find a new way—and a new place—to live.

Despite this feeling of alienation from the kitchen, Sunée does not abandon the space entirely. In fact, what is interesting about the resolution of Sunée's text is that she does not simply reject the space, nor does she merely overtake the kitchen and displace these patriarchal figures. Rather, like Melucci, she finds a way to work within that space on her own terms. After the chapter "With Reservations," Sunée continues to express her unhappiness to the reader by recalling moments when she is unable to eat and unable to cook; it almost appears as though she has lost the strong connection that she once had with the kitchen.[17] She no longer couples every chapter with an accompanying recipe; in fact, of the fifteen chapters that follow "With Reservations," only five include recipes. However, for Sunée, forsaking the kitchen entirely is simply not an option: the space provides her with far too much comfort to be completely disregarded. Instead, what she must do is find a kitchen space that is truly her own. When she moves to a one-bedroom apartment, she writes of her return to food: "I begin to make my own bread, it's both therapeutic and inexpensive, and I eat lots of vegetable curries with rice" (253–54). She ends this chapter by remarking on her resolve to remain separated from Olivier: "So, I am determined not to be defeated. I buy a baguette and slather it with butter and cheese, drink lots of coffee, as I concentrate on reading employment ads, following up on old contacts, and sending out my CV. Later, I will go to the market and buy beef, red wine, fresh herbs for a daube I haven't made since leaving the heart of Provence. I am determined to stay" (260). This chapter is one of the few that contains recipes at its close; here, it is a recipe for "La Daube Provençale." This chapter is appropriately titled "A Room of One's Own." In referencing Virginia Woolf's 1929 work that boldly declares, "a woman must have money and a room of her own if she is to write fiction," Sunée underscores for her reader how vital it is to her sense of self to carve out her own home space, occupying a kitchen not overseen by an oppressive presence. For Sunée, like Melucci, returning to the kitchen is only possible when she is settled in her own home.

This ability to feel settled and at home is not only tied to Sunée's reclamation of the kitchen, but it is also only possible when Sunée reconciles the conflicting feelings that she has about her cultural identity. She is not at ease in Louisiana, nor does she feel at home in Provence. Rather, for Sunée, home is found in the dishes that she cooks—dishes that expertly combine her cultural influences. As we've seen, throughout her memoir, Sunée writes of the tendency for people to label her whether it be as "Oriental" (by her classmates), "Chinetoque" (by Olivier's ex-wife), or "Américaine" (by friends in Corsica). In an interview with Tom Nolan, Sunée speaks of people's confusion regarding her heritage: "The French looked at me—Korean, from New Orleans, cooking and living in France—and they wanted to give me an identity. . . . You know, 'She's the American,' or 'She's the Asian-American.'" The recipes that Sunée includes in *Trail of Crumbs* directly counter these reductive views.

She includes recipes for food that speaks to her American heritage like crawfish bisque, for food that reflects her Korean heritage like kimchi soup, and for traditional French recipes like croque madame. Her memoir serves as both her autobiographical account of her search for and discovery of a home place and a cookbook devoid of any association with a particular regional cuisine. Additionally, many of her recipes locate a state of and/also, rather than either/or. The recipe for "French-Fry Po-Boy with Horseradish Crème Fraîche" puts a decidedly French continental flare on a Louisiana classic, speaking directly to the seemingly disparate backgrounds that Sunée learns to embrace. In her concluding chapter, "Hungry After All," she writes, "For now I have learned that home is in my heart—in all the places and people I have left behind. It's in the food that I cook and share with others, in the cities I will come to know, and in the offerings of street vendors around the world—from South Korea to Provence—in the markets I have yet to discover" (360). It is through this food that Sunée has finally found a sense of home.

In June 2019, K. T. Hawbaker published "How Nigella Lawson and Ina Garten Helped Me Love My Fat, Queer Self." In her essay, they write, "So often, women and femmes are made to separate their pleasure from their power, but Lawson keeps them both close at hand and uses food to bring them together."[18] Hawbaker found themselves interrogating their relationship with food the summer before their first year of college when their boyfriend admitted he had a fat fetish. The implication, Hawbaker (who already had body image issues) reasoned was that their boyfriend was dating them because of their larger body size. Hawbaker's article continues outlining their eating issues, noting that they loved food and "preached *hard* about the powerful, political relationships between women, femmes, non-binary people, and food, all while quietly having an affair with diet culture."

Like Melucci and Sunée, Hawbaker's essay presents readers with an individual struggling to accept the fact that food can provide them with pleasure and empowerment on their own terms.

Hawbaker notes that her relationship with her appetite changed with the help of Nigella Lawson and Ina Garten. They connect Garten's love for her husband with Garten's love for food, noting, "Garten looked at her husband like she looked at dessert—she and Jeffrey are wild about each other." Hawbaker concludes, "Ina somehow mastered what I'd been longing for all along: an unapologetic appetite, a body that took up ample space, an eager desire to love and be loved on equal terms, and an ability to show all that through food." Likewise, they reflect on the connection between Lawson's appetites when they write, "What I see in Lawson is a woman who is very plugged into how food, sex, and pleasure all overlap." They cite Lawson's recipe for "Slut Red Raspberries in Chardonnay Jelly" as an example.[19]

Hawbaker ultimately concludes that "resistance to oppressive gender roles begins in the kitchen." Lawson, in a 2018 article for Lena Dunham's now defunct *Lenny Letter*, agrees. In her reflection on home cooking titled "Nigella Lawson: Home Cooking Can Be a Feminist Act," she notes that very often home cooks are not given the accolades they deserve simply because they are engaging in a "feminine" act. She notes, "I have always felt that to disparage an activity because it has been traditionally female is itself anti-feminist." Lawson, like Melucci and Sunée, sees cooking as "one of the basic prerequisites for sustaining the self: it is an act of primary independence." In acknowledging and accepting their appetites and feeding themselves in their own spaces and on their own terms, these women cooks and writers encourage readers to rethink the gender politics of the kitchen.

5

THE GENDER POLITICS OF MEAT

The Foodie Romance and Julie Powell's *Cleaving*

In 2009, Julie Powell—best known for blogging about cooking her way through Julia Child's 1961 *Mastering the Art of French Cooking*—wrote a second memoir titled *Cleaving: A Story of Marriage, Meat, and Obsession* (2009). While Powell had successfully adapted her blog into a book (*Julie & Julia: 365 Days, 524 Recipes, 1 Tiny Apartment Kitchen*, 2005) and then had her book adapted into a film, *Julie & Julia* (2009), starring Meryl Streep and Amy Adams, *Cleaving* did not receive such acclaim. The book details Powell's affair, her separation from her husband Eric, and her attempts to heal herself through an apprenticeship to a family-owned butcher in the Catskills. Of the 201 customer reviews on Amazon, 50 percent are one star ("*Cleaving: A Story of Marriage, Meat, and Obsession*"). Reader reviews have such titles as "Don't bother with this cheap read" (Carrie) and "Save Yourself! It should be ZERO stars" (Christel S. Hachigian). The content of their reviews is even more disparaging:

"Can it possibly be this easy to get published? Write some garbage about butchering. . . . that will almost turn you into a vegetarian . . . cheat on your husband. . . . stalk. . . . lie and drink to excess . . . and there you have it. . . . a book worth publishing. Really?" (mk). Another reviewer expresses disappointment that this book does not fulfill the expectations he had after having read *Julie & Julia*: "So disappointing, after the brilliant first book, in which we readers revelled [*sic*] in the brilliantly depicted marriage relationship as much or more than the cooking, cubicle-dwelling, and blogging, to have to slog through this painful recitation of selfishness, skanky adultery, and flowering alcoholism. If you loved *Julie & Julia*, skip this one, and preserve your pleasant memories" (Thomas W. Allen).

Critics agreed. Like readers, professional book reviewers often focus on how "unlikeable" Powell presents herself to her readers. Writing for the *A. V. Club*, Tasha Robinson observes, "[Powell] comes across as callow and far too pleased with herself, particularly when describing how she assumes other people see her, as beautiful, rakish, mysterious, and—in a bit of purple prose far more stomach-turning than the descriptions of chopping up animals—possibly just a bit *dangerous*." *New York Times* writer Christine Muhlke warns potential readers, "The squeamish—morally or otherwise—should read elsewhere" (B30). Other reviews criticize the "messiness" of the text itself. Writing for *Time*, Mary Pols characterized the book as "a ghastly work of revelation without enough self-reflection." NPR's Linda Holmes elaborates on this idea: "[P]erspective is what *Cleaving* doesn't have, perhaps because it seems to have been written with great haste (the timeline dictates as much, really) as it was happening, without the benefit of the kind of distance that a story like this requires. It's just tell, tell, tell."

Despite these negative reviews, I find Powell's *Cleaving* to be redeeming for the way in which it critiques the gender politics of food consumption and preparation. While her memoir *Julie & Julia* recounts moments of home cooking intertwined with stories of her supportive husband, *Cleaving* centers on Julie's separation from

The Foodie Romance and Julie Powell's *Cleaving*   91

Eric and her attempt to make sense of her marriage by serving as an apprentice to a butcher in upstate New York. At this shop (Fleisher's), Powell learns the art of butchery while simultaneously working out her feelings for her lover, a man only known as D.[1] In her relationship with D, Julie is completely passive, at the whim of D's desires rather than her own. The narrative tension of *Cleaving* rests with Powell's attempts to position herself as the consumer, or empowered, rather than as an object to be consumed. In doing so, Powell calls attention to the gender politics of meat preparation and consumption and deconstructs what literary critic Jessica Lyn Van Slooten has labeled the genre of the "foodie romance"—the genre to which *Julie & Julia* belongs.

Central to Powell's narrative are the connections that she makes between sex and butchery. The most obvious is the parallel plotlines of her affair with D and her apprenticeship at the butcher shop Fleisher's. She also draws subtler connections, however. Sausages remind Powell of penises, the clod is called "the money cut" (162), and the butchers perform such acts as "frenching," "boning," and "peeling out skirts." She also consistently compares herself to animals throughout her memoir. For instance, she uses the command "heel" (23), commonly associated with a dog, in reference to herself; later, she returns to this dog comparison when she describes herself as lapping up water (256).

Powell not only likens herself to an animal, but she will often describe her own body in butchery terms. When recalling a sexual encounter with D, she recalls, "*his mouth moving unhurriedly down my flank toward what he wants to be doing*" (64), using the term "flank" calls to mind images of the meat that Powell describes butchering; later, she explains that D is "a breast man" (56). When learning the art of butchery, she finds it helpful to image the animal in human terms: "Pigs' cheeks are just like our cheeks, fleshy rounds. Feel along on your own face, if you like, as I describe: cutting from the hinge of the jawbone, dig the knife up under the ridge of the cheekbone down to the arc of the upper teeth, curving around just short of the corner of the mouth, and back under, following the jawline again to the hinge" (102). Later, she writes, "Every steer that comes into the shop arrives broken into eight pieces, called 'primals.' The best way to picture these primals is to use your own body as a sort of guide. First, hang yourself by a hook upside down, gut yourself, take off your head, and cut yourself in half vertically" (157). In both examples, Powell makes a direct comparison between the animal that she is breaking down and a human being.

In these moments, when Powell is connecting herself to animals, she is also reinforcing the association of women with animals. Powell herself is female, and the intended audience for both *Cleaving* and her earlier book, *Julie & Julia*, is female. The "you," then, becomes gendered as the reader images herself gutted and cut in half. Writing in the first person also allows the female reader to identify with the narrative voice. This connection between women and animals is the topic of Carol J. Adams's 1990 manifesto *The Sexual Politics of Meat* and her subsequent work, *The Pornography of Meat* (2003). Adams outlines the ways in which—historically—animals and women have been linked. Both books contain a large number of images in which animals and women are confused. For instance, Adams analyzes an image of an anthropomorphized turkey in an ad for a "turkey hooker" (a utensil that makes moving a turkey from pan to plate much easier) (108). The turkey is feminized; she is wearing heels, and her breasts are accentuated. She's also posed in what Adams calls "the pose of a hooker," one arm (or wing) up with the hand resting on the head. In another ad for University Row, the woman is present but assumes the position of a tiger (41). She's trapped in a cage while a nattily dressed man stands outside and above her. The correlation between animals and women are made clear in both images.

The reasoning for this conflation, Adams argues, is that both animals and women serve as "absent referents." People, she notes, need "intellectual and emotional separation" from the animal they are eating in order to consume meat (51). When women become the absent referent, it is much easier to treat them like objects—or

The Foodie Romance and Julie Powell's *Cleaving*   93

animals. And part of that treatment is to exhibit dominance and even aggression. As Adams notes, "Men *act*; women *appear*. Men are strong; women are strong temptations" (129). Here is where Adams expands upon the idea that by correlating women and animals we are sanctioning sexual violence. In revisiting the image described above of the woman in a cage, the man is dressed in a shirt and tie while the woman is scantily clad in a leopard print piece that reveals her shoulders and legs. In another advertisement from Adams's book for Think Skateboards, a man rests his feet on a woman who is on all fours. The man is fully dressed; the woman is in a bikini, a seductive gaze on her face. These images, Adams argues, make reference to the industry of pornography—an industry that often dehumanizes and victimizes women. When women are thought of as something other than human—as "meat," if you will—that gives the aggressor, usually male, the "intellectual and emotional separation" that they need to commit violent acts. These also uphold dominant/subordinate binaries valued in American culture such as man/woman, culture/nature, human/animal, white/people of color, and mind/body (39).

One of the most striking images in *The Sexual Politics of Meat* is from *Playboar*, which Adams notes is "a magazine that calls itself 'the pig farmer's *Playboy*'" (50). Adams describes the image:

A healthy sexual being poses near her drink: she wears bikini panties only and luxuriates on a large chair with her head rested seductively on an elegant lace doily. Her inviting drink with a twist of lemon awaits on the table. Her eyes are closed; her facial expression beams pleasure, relaxation, enticement. She is touching her crotch in an attentive, masturbatory action. Anatomy of seduction: sex object, drink, inviting room, sexual activity. The formula is complete. But a woman does not beckon. A pig does. (50)

Here, the pig assumes the pose that—in mainstream pornography—might be taken by a woman. In this image, the pig and the woman are not only interchangeable but both available.

In her books, Adams consistently reminds the reader that equating women to animals reinforces hegemonic masculinity; when women are seen as passive, men become the actors. Powell echoes this equation in *Cleaving*, consistently asserting that the ones wielding the tools (usually men) are the dominant ones. For instance, when writing about the meat hook, she notes: "(Funny, about meat hooks, I've had the phrase *meat hooks* in my vocabulary for as long as I can remember, accompanied by the vision of a broad-chested, letter-jacketed thug pawing at a comely bobby-soxer)" (31). Here, a man uses his "meat hooks" to assert his authority over a woman. Powell complicates this image, making it even more horrific, with the following lines: "Actually, using this meat hook, a sharp, small, thin tool that fits so coolly and easily in the palm, provokes a tiny, almost imperceptible shift of perspective. Meat hooks aren't like 'meat hooks' at all. They're much more effective and terrifying" (31). While Powell was previously troubled by the image, her horror is amplified when she understands just what the meat hook looks like and how it is used. And, while she doesn't explicitly provide the reader with an image associated with this new understanding of the tool as she did with the "letter-jacketed thug" and the "comely bobby-soxer," the reader can imagine how much more horrific a violation would be with this "sharp, small, thin tool."

Fleisher's butcher shop is a space imbued by hegemonic masculinity. Fleisher's employees are predominantly male, and the men in that space consistently perform their gender in stereotypical ways.[2] There is locker-room talk, insults such as "pussy" being hurled, and a pornography mixtape that plays while meat is broken down. They seem insistent on asserting their manhood whether it be through competitions regarding who can break down meat the fastest or through assigning Powell tasks that they think might gross her out.

The passages where male/dominant and female/submissive binaries are most noticeable are when Powell describes her sexual encounters with D. She writes, "This is where we should be having the Fight Sex. Where I say something sufficiently angry, petulant,

The Foodie Romance and Julie Powell's *Cleaving*   95

ultimatum-y, that leaves nothing for him to do but flip me over and fuck the living daylights out of me—doggy-style" (57). Later, she remembers, "The first time he slapped me across the face, after all, I was bound in trusses *I'd* given him"; here, Powell equates herself with the meat that she herself is learning to truss up (80). Powell's memories of her affair often focus first on the initial exhilaration that she felt; she thrillingly recalls, "He slapped my ass, bit me, hard, left bruises all over my body that I had to take care to hide, dark and mottled" (80). Of the slap scene, Powell writes that she felt "emancipated" after it happened (80). But these passages frequently end with her realization that this thrill was only temporary. Just a few sentences after her recollection of the slap, she writes, "But now he's gone, and it turns out my freedom was only probationary" (80). These moments with D are not, for Powell, empowering—though they may first seem to be; rather, she finds them to be ultimately degrading. And, when D eventually calls things off, Powell becomes increasingly disgusted with her behavior as she calls and texts him incessantly and even has sex with a stranger, immediately texting D afterward in order to provoke some sort of reaction.

Jovian Parry's article "Gender and Slaughter in Popular Gastronomy" for *Feminism & Psychology* is one of the few essays that analyzes *Cleaving* at length. He begins by referencing Adams's theories of animals and meat eating when discussing popular cooking shows such as *The F Word*, *Kiwi Kitchen*, and *Jamie's Great Italian Escape* before turning to the gender politics in *Cleaving*. Parry's chief concern rests with the way in which Powell adopts the traditionally masculine art of butchery in order to exert control over her irrational, feminine self. He states, "By transforming a natural (former)-subject into a cultural artefact, she imposes order on the natural world, and all that world represents, including the elements of her own personality that tend to get filed under animal/nature/body" (390). He continues, "In addition to appropriately channeling the unruly desires of the female body by dismembering the bodies of non-humans, *Cleaving* presents butchery as a means of subverting and challenging traditional gender stereotypes of women as inherently delicate or prim" (391). Ultimately, Parry argues, "Powell affirms her own status as truly human by butchering animals, demonstrating her equal competence in a traditionally male-dominated profession and asserting her right to consume high-status food products traditionally associated with men" (392).

To me, Powell's attraction to the art of butchery represents much more than her desire to exude control over her irrational, feminine self. While Parry rather nicely articulates the ways in which Powell's apprenticeship proves empowering—that is, situates her in the male-dominated profession of butchery—he seems to underestimate the culturally significant connections between women and animals. Parry is correct in his observation that meat, or "high-status food products" are "traditionally associated with men" (392). In a 1905 article for *Ladies Home Journal* titled "Men and Meat," the author encourages readers to reduce the amount of red meat in the diets of their men. More significantly, the author establishes the long-held belief that red meat is equal to strength: "It is the hardest thing, as women have found out, to convince the average American man that he eats too much red meat. . . . He is firmly convinced that the more red meat he eats the stronger he will be. And so he stows away a chop for breakfast, roast beef at midday, and steak for his evening meal" (16). Such discourse helped to establish the belief that real men were meat eaters and that their power was linked to the consumption of this food. In his article "Men, Meat, and Marriage: Models of Masculinity" for *Food and Foodways*, Jeffery Sobal also observes that meat eating is associated with strong, virile men. He links this meat eating with the (largely) masculine practice of hunting. "Vegetarianism," he notes, "provides an identity that transgresses masculinity in Western societies" (141). Hank Rothgerber's article "Real Men Don't Eat (Vegetable) Quiche: Masculinity and the Justification of Meat Consumption" also supports this assumption, going so far as to show the ways in which popular culture feminizes vegetarianism. He begins his article with a quote from

The Foodie Romance and Julie Powell's *Cleaving*   97

the popular men's magazine *Men's Health*: "Vegetables are for girls. If your instincts tell you following a vegetarian diet isn't manly, you're right." In his study, Rothgerber finds, "The relative lack of male enthusiasm for animal rights and vegetarianism may best be understood as an outgrowth of masculinity itself" (364).

In equating herself with animals, then, Powell is playing into these gender politics. Animals (women) are to be consumed by hunters (men); the consumption of this meat reinforces the hunters' (men's) power. When describing her sexual encounters with D, Powell often makes these comparisons and, in doing so, characterizes her relationship with D as disempowering, despite her claim that she likes "a bit of the rough and tumble" (92). She is the animal; he is the hunter. She is the submissive; he is the dominant. She is the consumed; he is the consumer. Like Parry, I see Powell's participation in the art of butchery as empowering, but I would also argue that her participation in butchery becomes an attempt at correcting these disempowering sexual experiences with D. Powell doesn't simply want to assert her humanity by butchering animals; rather, she wants to reposition herself from her role as a disempowered object to an empowered woman with sexual agency.

The turning point of Powell's memoir is not when she finishes her apprenticeship at Fleisher's. Rather, the turning point happens later in the memoir—a moment in the text that Parry does not analyze in his article. Having returned home to New York City and Eric, Powell still doesn't feel settled and plans a trip to Buenos Aries. When that trip still doesn't heal her, she embarks on a journey to Ukraine and Tanzania with a brief final stopover in Japan. While in Tanzania, she shares a romantic moment with Elly, one of the guides. That night, a man who had witnessed their interaction comes into Powell's tent not once but twice, sexually assaulting her and attempting to rape her. Powell's reaction to this event is unsettling. She doesn't want to get the man in trouble: "*I'm being a castrating bitch. . . . I'm ruining this guy's life*" (273). Later, she writes the same account of the incident in letters to both D and Eric: "*I think I thought this was what I'd earned. For all that I've done or felt over the last few years. In my half-awake animal brain, I deserved this. Even when I finally, finally got up the gumption to hit him, I kept my voice to a whisper. Even when I made him leave, even when I told my story, even when I was in the ranger station and the guy was being questioned, some little-girl piece of me figured this was my fault"* (279). The guilt and shame that Powell has been carrying around with her about her affair, the sexual encounters, and her marriage all come to a head in this passage. In her *"animal brain,"* she thinks that this is the way that women deserve to be treated—that this is the role that women play. When she returns to New York, she has a dream in which she can finally scream—an indication that she has found her voice, resisting a patriarchy that consistently defines her as female/animal/submissive.

Powell's inclusion of recipes in her memoir reinforces her movement away from the role of consumed and toward the role of consumer. Throughout *Cleaving*, Powell includes recipes for skirt steak salad, braised pork cheeks, and short ribs; these recipes accompany those chapters in which she is learning about the technique for breaking down these cuts of meat. Powell not only knows how to break down the meat that she recommends using for these recipes, but she also frequently writes of her enjoyment of the food. Many of the recipes are credited to the people she works with at the butcher: "Jessica's Super Easy Skirt Steak Salad," for instance, or "Juan's Mother's Blood Sausage." Interestingly enough, she includes two of her husband's recipes. They are the beginning and ending recipes. There is no recipe, however, attributed to D. With this recipe selection, Powell seems to banish the hunter; instead, she is the one providing, preparing, and consuming the meat.

At the start of each chapter, there is a small, meat-centered illustration by Diana Cone. Some are full cuts of meat; one is a meat grinder. Two images, in particular, are striking in comparison to one another and to other meat imagery that's been explored in this chapter. The first is an illustration at the start of chapter 12 of a cow

The Foodie Romance and Julie Powell's *Cleaving*   99

whose body is drawn in a way that delineates each section of the animal. This chapter chronicles Powell's time in Buenos Aires, and the animal is labeled using the Spanish equivalent for these sections—for example, *cogote* (nape), *nalga de adentro* (inside buttock), and *matambre* (flank steak but the literal translation is slaughter). The second image is found at the beginning of chapter 9; this image is of a man—his body marked up in the same way as the cow's. Both of these images recall other animal iconography, such as the cover illustration of Adams's text or actress and vegetarian Pamela Anderson's 2010 PETA ad. Clad in a bikini, Anderson's body is marked up just as a butcher might mark up a piece of meat—with labels such as round, rump, and ribs (Jones "Pamela Anderson Poster"). However, the second image encapsulates "the imperceptible shift of perspective" that Powell speaks of in her meat hook passage. While the image might remind the reader of previous animal iconography, the image is not of an animal or a woman; it's of a man, trussed up, bound at the feet, and hanging upside down. It is his body, not the body of an animal or a woman, who is dissected for the reader. The image signals that no longer is Powell positioned in the role of the hunted, the submissive, and trussed up. Rather, she has exchanged her trusses for a butcher knife, thus exchanging her previous role of the hunted and consumed for the role of hunter and consumer.

Powell's switch in position from submissive to dominant, passive to active, object to subject takes on a larger significance when thinking about the gender politics of the kitchen—both in the public and private spheres. The restaurant industry has long been notorious for its gender discrimination. Ann Cooper, in her book *"A Woman's Place Is in the Kitchen": The Evolution of Women Chefs* (1997), devotes a good deal of her book to discussing the inequities in the restaurant industry, particularly the fact that there is such a small representation of women chefs: "As of February 1997, of the 2,134 certified executive chefs (currently active) practicing their craft in the United States, only 92 are women. . . . That represents 4.3 percent, a far cry from what you'd expect to see in an industry where cooking was traditionally a woman's domain" (86).[3] Several years later, the Restaurant Opportunities Centers United, whose mission "is to improve wages and working conditions for the nation's low-wage restaurant workforce," continued to report on gender discrimination in the restaurant industry ("About Us"). In February 2012, the organization published the report "Tipped over the Edge—Gender Inequity in the Restaurant Industry," noting "restaurants' most lucrative roles are dominated by men—only 19 percent are women." Six years later, a 2018 article for *The Observer* corroborates these findings. Clarissa Buch writes: "The stats regarding women in the culinary space are pretty grim. Only 33 percent of restaurants are majority owned by women, says Dawn Sweeney, President of the National Restaurant Association. According to Grubhub—who recently launched a website to promote female-owned restaurants—only 19 percent of chefs are women. That number shrinks to just 7 percent when accounting for head chefs." Instead, women appear in large numbers in service positions. So, even though as Rewards Network reports, "there are nearly equal numbers of men and women working in the industry, we still see pockets of the industry today where 7 out of 10 servers, but only 2 out of 10 chefs, are women."

These service positions, which are predominantly occupied by women, historically have promised very little pay. In "Tipped over the Edge," ROC-United notes that the payment for these server positions has been "frozen at only $2.13 per hour for the past 20 years," which has greatly contributed to "poverty for these working women." Then, in 2015, ROC-United published "Ending Jim Crow in America's Restaurants: Racial and Gender Occupational Segregation in the Restaurant Industry," which asserted, "today restaurant works are effectively separated by race and gender by a partition between livable-wage and poverty-wage positions. . . . [R]estaurant workers occupy seven of the ten lowest paid occupations reported by the Bureau of Statistics, and the economic position of workers of color in the restaurant industry is particularly precarious." In that study, which focused on California, the state with the largest restaurant industry, one of the key findings showed that "[t]he greatest racial and gender wage inequality is in the highest wage occupational categories—namely fine-dining server and bartender position."[4] Again, Buch substantiates this point regarding economic disparity, noting "women working in restaurants earn 28 percent less in base pay than their male counterparts."

Women in the restaurant industry have challenges in addition to lack of representation and equal pay; they also, as the ROC-United reports, "face systematic discrimination, poverty wages, a lack of sick days, and five times more harassment than the general female workforce." Shortly after the rise of the #MeToo movement in late 2017, which mobilized in alliance with the women who brought sexual assault allegations against film producer Harvey Weinstein, the *Harvard Business Review* examined sexual harassment in the restaurant industry. They reference high-profile cases involving such men as restaurant owner Ken Friedman, *The Great American Baking Show* judge (and pastry chef) Johnny Iuzzini, and celebrity chef Mario Batali.[5] They also note, "More sexual harassment claims in the U.S. are filed in the restaurant industry than in any other, where as many as 90% of women and 70% of men reportedly experience some form of sexual harassment" (Johnson and Madera). The article goes on to outline the ways in which the infrastructure of the restaurant industry allows for this harassment to occur, including the gender configuration of the "front of house" and "back of house" jobs, the reliance on tips, and the industry's implicit belief that the customer is always right.

These issues of gender discrimination become amplified as when subsets of the restaurant industry are examined—particularly the field of butchery that has been a field predominantly occupied by men. Reporting for NPR's *The Salt*, Leoneda Inge interviews Kari Underly, a master butcher from Chicago. Underly explains the reasons for this male domination: "'Meat production has always been a male job, just because of the sheer size,' of the animals involved. . . .

'It's a physical job—actually being able to lift these large animals.'" Writing of her own experience as a butcher, Melissa Cortina noted that in 2010, the National Women's Law Center estimated "only 24.6% of individuals working full-time as butcher or meat-cutters were women." For 2016, *DATA USA* reported the following statistics for butchers and other meat, poultry, and fish processing workers ("Butchers and Other Meat, Poultry, and Fish Processing Workers"). First, they indicated that 78.2% of workers in this field are male. In terms of salary, the average salary is $28,725; on average, men make $30,147 while women make $23,629 ("Butchers and Other Meat, Poultry, and Fish Processing Workers"). More recent statistics from the *Boston Globe* in 2017 indicate that 26.9 percent of all "butchers and other meat, poultry, and fish processing workers were women" (Rocheleau).[6] In recording her experiences in this male-dominated field, Powell encourages reflection on the way in which the public kitchen has included and excluded women.

In *Julie & Julia*, Powell created for the reader what Kathleen Anne McHugh in *American Domesticity: From How-To Manual to Hollywood Melodrama* (1999) describes as the domestic: "home, family, maternity, warmth, hearth, to the creation of a private place where we can be who we really are, to a set of experiences, possessions, and sentiments that are highly symbolically valued in our culture" (6). In *Cleaving*, she deconstructs the home kitchen that played a central role in her earlier memoir. While in *Julie & Julia*, Powell transgressed domestic expectations in some ways (she curses like a sailor throughout the narrative and often makes a mess of some of the recipes), the space that she writes of is relatively peaceful; it's a space that includes a devoted husband and a stable marriage. The Powell in *Cleaving*, however, is one who has abandoned delusions of domestic bliss. Instead, she actively destroys her marriage.

Jessica Lyn Van Slooten, in "A Marriage Made in the Kitchen: Amanda Hesser's *Cooking for Mr. Latte* and Julie Powell's *Julie & Julia* as Foodie Romance," labels Powell's earlier work "foodie romance." Van Slooten characterizes this genre as one that "capitalize[s] on the

The Foodie Romance and Julie Powell's *Cleaving*   103

. . . romance, chick lit, and foodie memoir trends" and "chronicle[s] the pleasures and complications of relationships and consumption." Many of these texts (for example, Hesser's *Cooking for Mr. Latte* and Elizabeth Bard's *Lunch in Paris: A Love Story, with Recipes*) adopt classic romance tropes. *Cleaving* responds to these texts by detailing the dissolution of a marriage—not the fairytale romance— simultaneous with Powell's learning the very grisly art of butchering. In doing so, Powell removes herself from the home kitchen and the domestic act of food preparation, exchanging it for the public space of the butcher shop and the traditionally male-dominated art of butchery. Her experience in the public kitchen at Fleisher's becomes the way in which she tentatively repairs her homelife and, in turn, her home kitchen. The end of *Cleaving* promises some hope of reconciliation with her husband.[7]

Despite it being a little over a decade since *The Pornography of Meat*'s publication, popular culture images in which animals are equated with women are still prevalent. Ludacris's 2003 album *Chicken-n-Beer* features the rap artist in front of a table filled with chicken, about to bite into the leg of a woman. Another example is Pamela Anderson's previously mentioned PETA ad. This messaging is present on television as well as in HBO's *True Detective: Season One* (2014) and HBO's more recent *Sharp Objects* (2018). The premise of the first show is a revisiting of a 1995 murder in which a dead, naked prostitute is found in a prayer position with deer antlers on her head. Nearly twenty years later, another woman is found in the same position, sparking interest in the earlier case, which was claimed to have been solved. In *Sharp Objects*, the protagonist Camille Preaker (Amy Adams) revisits her hometown when a young girl goes missing; the show toggles back and forth between Camille's childhood and the current narrative. In the series premiere, "Vanish," a young Camille stumbles across a shed; pornographic photos are displayed on the walls, and meat is hanging from the ceiling and drying on the table.[8] While one might argue that linking animals and humans might help people to better identify with and, subsequently, reject animal cruelty or that both *True Detective* and *Sharp Objects* draw attention to heinous crimes against women, the sexual element confuses these messages.[9] Instead, they reproduce the messages about animals, women, sex, and violence that Carol Adams draws her readers' attention to. In adopting the tools of the butcher, Powell reclaims a sense of power that she lost with D. *Cleaving* becomes a site of resistance, an "emancipatory counter-discourse," that stands in opposition to the dangerous messaging that positions women as the hunted and men as the hunters.

6

BLOG HER

Transgressing Narrative Boundaries

On 2 March 2012, Eliza Barclay reported to NPR's readers of *The Salt*, NPR's food blog, on the Hartman Group and Publicis Consultants USA's study titled *Clicks & Cravings: The Impact of Social Technology on Food Culture*. The Hartman Group, Barclay writes, is "a consumer research firm, and Publicis Consultants USA, a marketing agency." The groups "used a combination of in-depth interviews and a national phone survey to probe the ways that social media is changing food culture." Barclay discusses their chief finding: "In essence, they found that social media is becoming deeply embedded in our food habits: Half of consumers use sites like Twitter and Facebook to learn about food. Another 40 percent of consumers say they learn about food via websites, apps, or blogs." Barclay's article is titled "Bloggers Replace Mom's Recipe Box as Source of Food Knowledge."

While online readers of Barclay's article note that the groups' findings are interesting, many who posted about it either on their own blogs or in *The Salt*'s comment section after the article countered the reductive title. On the site theKitchn, Megan Gordon, reflecting on Barclay's piece, wrote, "But I can't let print go. I love flipping through cookbooks and I cherish my mom's recipes jotted down on old scratch papers. Call me an optimist, but I do feel that print recipes still hold a lot of weight." In the comments section after Barclay's article, one reader, Basilmomma/Heather Tallman wrote, "This is very interesting. As a food blogger and food columnist, I do still go to paper cookbooks for ideas." Another, Marita Madeloni, commented, "I do follow a lot of blogs but also love my cookbooks and family recipes. . . . Those recipes and the stories behind them are what get me excited about cooking and eating!" And, in fact, the executive summary of the report itself includes findings that complicate the assertion that cooking blogs are replacing cookbooks. For instance, the report reads, "When asked if they spend more time reading about food from print vs. online sources, 46% of online consumers say they spend more time engaged online vs. 31% who say they are equally engaged in online and print." The discrepancy is not as significant as Barclay's title belies.

NPR reader EthanDreamer/Ethan Carter's comment regarding Barclay's article is perhaps the most telling. He writes in response to another reader, who expresses concern that people no longer value print culture: "[N]obody is 'throwing out' Mom's/Grandma's recipes. They are just being *augmented* [my emphasis] with other recipes." In choosing the word augmented rather than replaced, Carter dispels the myth that one can only exist without the other, embracing the and/also instead of the either/or. Carter's comment entertains the possibility that, instead of displacing the recipe box, the laptop and the index cards can rest side-by-side on the kitchen counter.

Throughout *Season to Taste*, we have seen multiple examples of US Americans' strong compulsion to embrace binaries: public/private, masculine/feminine, feminist/housewife. The title of NPR's online article reinforces these divides as well, adding print/online to the mix. In this chapter, I will discuss the ways in which food bloggers explore similar themes as print food memoirists. However, structurally, the medium of the blog blurs genre lines between diaries, food memoirs, and cookbooks. Specifically, I will look at two early adopters of the blog genre—Molly Wizenberg, who began her site *Orangette* in July 2004 as a place to begin writing for herself, and Shauna James Ahern, Wizenberg's fellow Pacific Northwesterner and author of the blog *Gluten-Free Girl*, who began recording her struggle with celiac disease a year later. Though both Wizenberg and Ahern record their experiences on a near-daily basis like diarists of the past, using recipes to punctuate their entries as food memoirists do, the structural qualities of the blog medium—from the reverse ordering of entries to the inclusion of photographs and hyperlinks to the interactions that the comments feature encourages between writer and reader—enable writers like Wizenberg and Ahern to disrupt the conventions of diaries, food memoirs, and cookbooks. Ultimately, Wizenberg's and Ahern's blogs complicate traditional genre forms and contribute a new chapter to the history of women and food writing.

In his review of Ben Yagoda's *Memoir: A History* for the *New Yorker*, Daniel Mendelsohn argues that the advent of the internet with its free self-publishing services like Blogger and WordPress has produced "The greatest outpouring of personal narratives in the history of the planet . . . as soon as there was a cheap and convenient means to do so, people enthusiastically paid to disseminate their autobiographies, commentaries, opinions, and reviews, happily assuming the roles of both author and publisher." As Jenn Watt reported in her article "Blogging Busts Out for Women," as early as 2006, women were among the blogosphere's most active participants. Watt writes, "Fifty-five percent of bloggers are women, according to blogher.com, a blog that encourages women bloggers through conferences and resources" (7). She continues, "And according to the feminist wire service *Women's E-News*, women start more blogs than men and are more likely to keep them going for a longer time" (7). In Watt's article, Natalie Bennett, founder of Carnival of Feminists, a site that "aims to build the profile of feminist blogging," explains the reasons she feels women are drawn to the genre:

"[Blogging] is, I think, inherently democratic. . . . Certainly, there are still economic and skills barriers to blogs, but large numbers of women—certainly in more developed countries, and increasingly in less developed—have access to blogging. And the fact that it can be anonymous gives [women] power to put their views out into the world and have them recognized" (7).

A testament to women's involvement in the blogging community at the start of the twenty-first century can be seen through the growth and development of BlogHer. BlogHer began in 2005, when Elisa Camahort, Jory Des Jardins, and Lisa Stone conceptualized a conference for women bloggers and women interested in blogging ("BlogHer Co-founders Lisa Stone, Elisa Camahort Page, and Jory Des Jardins among FORTUNE's 2013 Most Powerful Women Entrepreneurs"). The first conference, attended by around three hundred people, took place in San Jose, California.[1] Since then, the company has grown. Just two years after being founded, BlogHer made headlines in the *Media Report to Women* when "the Web's number-one guide to blogs by women, announced in October that the BlogHer Network now receives more than 4.23 million unique visitors per month" ("BlogHer Network Joins Ranks of Top Women's Networks Online"). The article continued, noting that BlogHer, at the time, currently comprised "955 blog affiliates" and "60 editors." As of the publication of *Season to Taste*, BlogHer "is a leading content and events platform with a mission to provide economic empowerment for all women" ("About Us"). They provide in-person and virtual events as well as "on-demand video and content library to feed an increasing demand for 24/7 small business education and inspiration" ("About Us"). According to the organization's "About Us" page, they reach "10M+ women business owners and decision-makers." BlogHer serves as the flagship site of SHE Media "a mission-driven digital media company created by and for women with 50+ million unique visitors per month and 350+ million social media fans and followers across the SHE Media Partner Network" ("#WeAreSHE").

The success of BlogHer's annual blogging conference demonstrates women's growing investment in online writing. At the first conference meeting, held in 2005, there were three hundred attendees, according to Elaine Wu, BlogHer's marketing and communications manager.[2] By contrast, Wu noted that at the 2012 conference, held in New York City, 5,100 people attended.[3] In addition, there were 130 sponsors of the event, a 30 percent increase over the number of sponsors in 2011. The 2012 conference included a host of sessions from technical workshops on how to best incorporate visual material into your blog to personal reflections on such topics as "mommy blogging" to professional speakers such as supermodel and "global maternal health advocate" Christy Turlington Burns and newswoman Katie Couric, who delivered a keynote speech. President Barack Obama even addressed the attendees of the three-day event in a live video. In 2019, BlogHer celebrated its fifteen-year anniversary with its conference in Brooklyn, and as of this printing, due to the global pandemic, BlogHer has been hosting genre-specific, online conference offerings, including conferences focused on both food and the planet.

Wu explained that one of the strongest subsets of the BlogHer Network rests with the area of food blogs. She noted that the BlogHer Food Network is "the #3 online food property in the U.S. (comScore, Apr. 2012), and four of the top five 'favorite food blogs,' selected by the general population from a diverse list of larger food blogs, are from the BlogHer Network." In fact, food blogging is so popular among users of BlogHer that in 2009 the network began the BlogHer Food conference—the second offshoot of the larger conference.[4] The first food blogging conference held in San Francisco had such strong attendance that subsequent gatherings have followed (San Francisco, 2010; Atlanta, 2011; Seattle, 2012). As of this printing, the most recent event (May 2019) took place in Brooklyn. The enthusiasm that BlogHer participants have shown for food blogging is not particular to that organization; food blogging has widespread appeal among the general public. As noted earlier, in her *Food Blogs, Postfeminism, and the Communication of Expertise: Digital Domestics*, Alane L. Presswood estimates the total number of active food bloggers at the time of the publication of her book in 2020 to be upward of 20,000 (1).

Presswood also remarked that women's participation in this online forum is strong and estimated that 85 percent of these food blogs are authored by women (44)—a statistic that is not surprising given women's investment in both writing cookbooks and auto-biographical writing.[5] While male food writers are certainly repre-sented in the blogosphere (see, for example, David Lebovitz at *David Lebovitz* or Michael W. Twitty at *Afroculinaria*), women have an equally strong presence and are becoming increasingly recognized for their work. For instance, in 2010, *Saveur*'s 1st Annual Food Blog Awards recognized nine blogs in nine different categories. Three of those blogs were authored by men, one was collectively written, and four were blogs by women.[6] The Bloggies, which have been deemed the Oscars of the blogosphere, has been acknowledging top blogs since 2005.[7] The results in the category Best Food Blog speak to women's presence in the field. Since the food blog award was first given in 2005, women have won this award eight of the eleven years.[8] Not only have we seen a strong and increasing presence of women food bloggers, but we have seen many of those women be recognized in their field for the exceptional work that they are doing.

The content of food blogs varies from blogs that focus on baking, cooking, and food photography to more specialized blogs that center exclusively on such things as bacon (for example, *The Bacon Show*) and bento box creations (for example, *Happy Little Bento: Making Cute, Healthy and Nutritious Bento for Kids*). The two food bloggers examined here, Molly Wizenberg, creator of *Orangette*, and Shauna James Ahern, of *Gluten-Free Girl*, began blogging around the same time; Wizenberg's first entry dates 29 July 2004, while Ahern began on 10 May 2005. Both women have become incredibly successful since those first posts. Wizenberg's blog was recognized as Best Overall Food Blog in the Well Fed Network 2005 Food Blog Awards (Jones

"The Food Blog That Sparked Delancey Celebrates 10 Years"). She was also awarded one of the fifty best food blogs in 2009 by the *London Times* (L. Robinson 2009). In 2015, she won the James Beard Award for Individual Food Blog in 2015 ("Chef: Molly Wizenberg") and has published three memoirs, *A Homemade Life: Stories and Recipes from My Kitchen Table* (2013), *Delancey: A Man, A Woman, A Restaurant, A Marriage* (2014), and *The Fixed Stars* (2020). Ahern's honors include her blog being recognized as one of the fifty best blogs in the world by the *London Times* (L. Robinson 2009) and one of the twenty best blogs by and for women in the world by the *Sunday Telegraph* ("Shauna Ahern: Founder and CEO, glutenfreegirl.com"). In 2014, she also received a James Beard Award for Focus on Health for her book *Gluten-Free Girl Every Day*, which she cowrote with her husband Daniel Ahern ("2014 Book Awards Recap"). In addition to this book, she has written two memoirs—*Gluten-Free Girl: How I Found the Food That Loves Me Back and How You Can Too* (2009) and *Enough: Notes from a Woman Who Has Finally Found It* (2020)—as well as cookbooks coauthored with her husband, chef Daniel Ahern (*Gluten-Free Girl and the Chef: A Love Story with 100 Tempting Recipes*, 2012 and *Gluten-Free Girl American Classics Reinvented*, 2015).

Thematically, Wizenberg's and Ahern's blogs are very similar to the food memoirs already discussed here. Most obviously, like these other writers, both Wizenberg and Ahern write about the role that food and their preparation of it play in their lives. In her first entry, dated 29 July 2004, Wizenberg explains to her readers the purpose of her blog. While at the time of the post she was enrolled in an anthropology PhD program, where she had hoped to examine the French social security system, she has made the life decision to alter her career plans considerably. Her blog will serve the following purpose:

This is my space to start writing for myself again, rather than for only . . . professors, advisors, students, grant committees, and the like. . . . I'm not going through with my Ph.D. I was perhaps the last to see it, but better late than never.

The alternate plan, as it currently stands: I will continue for the coming year, to write my Master's thesis, do lots and lots of writing, and stick my neck out. Next stop: food writing, or perhaps cookbook editing. *It faut que je sois fonceuse*, as those French say.

Just three entries later, she writes about and posts a recipe for "Gâteau au Citron"—"French-Style Yogurt Cake with Lemon"—with an accompanying photograph. She continues with this formula in subsequent entries, sharing stories, recipes, and photographs. Later entries often place food at the forefront, such as the entry dated 22 October 2004, where Wizenberg shares a recipe for zucchini frittata.

Ahern begins her blog with an explanation of her celiac disease; she notes on 10 May 2005 in her first entry, titled "Diagnosed with Celiac," "For the past few months, I've been in lousy pain." She explains that it was a long road to discovering the cure, but when she was finally able to name her disease and cut gluten from her diet, she felt miraculously better. Her blog, then, becomes a way to share her journey with others. About a month after beginning her blog, Ahern records her first attempt at gluten-free cooking: gluten-free bread in a newly purchased bread machine. Though the result was less than desirable at first, by the end of the post, she shares with readers that she found an acceptable alternative to bread that's fulfilling. Before long, Ahern was uploading photographs of such homemade creations as her raspberry jam.

Wizenberg and Ahern also reflect on the space of the kitchen in their blogs, noting how they must make that space themselves to suit their needs. In a post titled "On Sharing and Sugar, with a Lot of Banana Cake," Wizenberg writes, "Like so many others who love the warmth of the stove, I once thought that I wanted to be a chef." She goes on to chart her dalliances with the professional restaurant world, but she concludes, "It didn't feel right to plate a dish and watch it disappear into the faceless unknown with a waiter whose name I couldn't remember. Forget this back-of-the-house business; I wanted my house, where the dining room and the kitchen were one." Ahern writes in her post "Two Loves, Both a Bit Silly, But I'm Besotted," "My kitchen has been making me happy all summer long. I swing my hips as I dance in front of the stove, creating new concoctions, like the blackberry sauce recipe from last night that made me nearly moan and stamp my feet this evening as I actually ate it. . . . Good parties always happen in the kitchen, people leaning against the counters with food in their hands. Cluttered or clean, I'm always happy to be in my kitchen." Both Wizenberg and Ahern distance themselves from the professional kitchen that Reichl worked so hard to align herself with. Instead, both women identify with the home cook. Wizenberg's comment brings to mind the changing space of the kitchen, recorded in *Better Homes and Gardens*. Her kitchen is not set off from the rest of the house, but her "dining room and the kitchen are one." Likewise, Ahern does not characterize herself as a woman trapped in the kitchen; rather, she is cooking and enjoying the food that she makes with others in her kitchen.

As I explored in chapter 3, throughout her blog, Ahern acknowledges the food work of previous generations when she reflects on the kitschy sensibility of Erin McKenna's bakery. Wizenberg, too, resists distancing herself from women of the past. Rather, she consistently acknowledges the food work of previous generations, much as Delk Adams does. Throughout her blog posts, a reader will find references to Julia Child ("Happily So") and Martha Stewart (Special Occasions, Special Measures") as well as fond memories of cooking with her mother ("To a Cherry-Pit Spitter on Her 58th") and father ("For a French Toast Master on His 76th"). And, like Melucci, Sunée, and Powell, these women articulate the ways in which cooking in their home kitchens are integral to their happiness. As Wizenberg explains, she no longer finds fulfillment in her graduate work and instead turns to her blog to write about what matters to her. In Ahern's case, she clearly loves her day job as a teacher, but she also notes, on more than one occasion, that she eagerly heads home each day to cook and then write about her creations. The space of the kitchen provides Wizenberg and Ahern with so much comfort, in fact, that they dedicate their daily lives to recording their adventures with food, and eventually each woman is able to leave their day jobs to pursue their passion for food and food writing full-time.

What is particularly interesting about the way in which Wizenberg and Ahern address these thematic issues regarding women, food, and the space of the kitchen is that they are electing to write in a genre that in and of itself pushes back on food-writing conventions. Structurally, blogs bear some resemblance to established genres, such as the diary, the food memoir, and the cookbook. But food blogs also transgress narrative conventions with elements such as hyperlinks and reader commenting, thus becoming a hybrid genre that blurs genre boundaries in addition to challenging such thematic binaries as masculine/feminine, feminist/housewife, producer/consumer, and public/private. In transgressing these narrative conventions, Wizenberg and Ahern use this hybrid genre form to further question cultural representations of women, the kitchen, and women's relationship to the food that they prepare and eat.

Blogs can be seen as the modern version of the diaries that women across centuries have been known for keeping. As Lena Karlsson writes in "Desperately Seeking Sameness: The Processes and Pleasures of Identification in Women's Diary Blog Reading," the Merriam-Webster dictionary first included a definition of the term "blog" in 2005, noting that a blog was "a Web site that contains an online personal journal with reflections, comments, and often hyperlinks provided by the writer" (138).[9] Like diaries, blogs "enable the writer to jot ideas in brief sittings and may also contain a great deal of repetition" (Brownley and Kimmich 149–50). In her 1980 essay "Towards a Theory of Form in Feminist Autobiography," Suzanne Juhasz theorizes that diary writing, "the classic verbal articulation of dailiness," was embraced by women because it reflects the structure of women's lives: "[W]omen's lives tend to be like the stories that they tell: they show less a pattern of linear development toward some clear goal than one of repetitive, cumulative, cyclical structure. One thinks of housework or childcare, of domestic life in general." Like diaries, blogs serve as a way for women to record the events of their lives and their impressions of those events.

Orangette and *Gluten-Free Girl* are both stylistically similar to traditional diaries. Each entry is dated, and in these entries, the bloggers meditate on their daily lives. In her first year of blogging, Wizenberg writes of a lamb roast with friends, the writers she admires, a David Byrne concert, and her birthday celebration. Likewise, Ahern writes about teaching, her friends, a gluten-free Thanksgiving, and the merits of a good knife. Wizenberg and Ahern post sporadically— sometimes daily, sometimes weekly—giving readers the impression that they write when they are able. Each blog, then, in its structure, draws upon the tradition of diary writing; these bloggers, like diarists, record their observations on a regular basis, capturing the substance of their daily lives.

Food blogs also resemble the genre of the cookbook. Both women's blogs include photographs of the food that they cook as well as recipes for their creations. In her first year of blogging, twenty-one of Wizenberg's sixty-two posts included recipes. By the end of the year, she was posting recipes with nearly every entry. Likewise, Ahern posts recipes of the gluten-free food that she experiments with in her kitchen. At first, Ahern is slow to start recording recipes, opting instead to describe the food that she is eating rather than provide directions on how to make it. On 28 July 2005, though, she posts her first recipe: "Apricot-Cherry Crisp." By August, her blogs more often than not follow the format of story followed by recipe. As their blogs evolve, both women include a link on their main pages titled "Recipes" so that readers can easily access instructions for the foods that Wizenberg and Ahern have made.

In these ways, then, Wizenberg and Ahern are drawing on the (female) literary traditions that came before them—both the diary and the cookbook. Yet, their blogs cannot quite be classified as one or the other; instead, their writing troubles traditional genre conventions and resists categorization of either/or. As Viviane Serfaty observes in *The Mirror and the Veil* (2004), blogs "extend and modify the traditional definition of the [diary] genre" (16). As much as the blog resembles the traditional diary and is often called an online journal, the format is different in significant ways. In her book, Serfaty acknowledges differences between the traditional diary and the blog such as the use of hyperlinks and multimedia. Additionally, blog entries are published backward, with the most recent entry being the first entry that the reader encounters when navigating the site. As a result, a reader will often begin at the ending of the blog, reading backward in time, getting to know the author and their work retrospectively. Unlike a diary, these blogs are published for an audience. Some diaries are published posthumously and thus become public; for example, diarists Anne Frank and Sylvia Plath, in their writing, were not conscious of an audience in the way that many bloggers are. Most bloggers—Wizenberg and Ahern included—leave their site open for people to stumble upon and read. Both Wizenberg and Ahern are aware of their audience and often write directly to their imagined public. Wizenberg's opening entry begins, "It's awfully quiet in here. If you're there, dear reader, welcome to the beginning," noting in the end, "We're off." Ahern signs her first post as she would a letter: "Love and a loaf of gluten-free bread." While one could argue that the public nature of the blog aligns the blog with the tradition of the food memoir, these blog entries do not have the polish of a print publication. Rather, they read as more informal. In writing each entry individually, there is not the type of narrative thread that there might be in a print memoir.

By adopting the structural similarities of the diary, the food memoir, and the cookbook and in deploying formal elements unique to the genre of the blog, these food blogs become what David Duff in *Modern Genre Theory* (2000) deems a hybrid genre. He defines a hybrid genre as such: "The process by which two or more genres combine to form a new genre or subgenre, or by which elements of two or more genres are combined into a single work" (xiv). Writing specifically of the hybrid memoir in "*Any Other Mouth*: Writing the Hybrid Memoir" (2017), Annalise McAdams notes, "[A] hybrid memoir is any memoir in which its author purposefully disrupts standard memoiristic convention in the telling of his or her own life, by using significant transgressions in content, style, or structure. As a result, the author will likely push generic boundaries, creating a text that may ultimately be difficult to categorise" (17). In form, blogs are a hybrid genre, blending and mixing traditional genre forms with nontraditional elements.[10]

Scholars of genre theory have noted that the "transformative power of in-between zones represented in literature" is what makes the hybrid genre so significant (van der Merwe and Viljoen 4). Vanessa Guignery, in her introduction to the anthology *Hybridity: Forms and Figures in Literature and the Visual Arts* (2011), writes, "The encounters and mixtures triggered off by hybrid processes open up new perspectives on the world and result in artistic forms that can combine different styles, languages, modes and genres" (3). For van der Merwe and Viljoen and Guignery, this mixing of genres becomes particularly powerful in the hands of marginalized groups, who, through their writing, are pushing back against the establishment not only with the ideas that they are presenting but also through the genre(s) in which they choose to write.

In her essay, "Gender and Genre" (1989), Mary Eagleton considered "the subversive potential of women's writing" (58), indicating that feminist, literary scholarship has considered "how women may transform the male-dominated forms" (58). In *An Alchemy of Genres: Cross-Genre Writing by American Feminist Poet-Critics* (1992), Diane P. Freedman speaks to the way in which women writers who blend or mix genres can push back against the patriarchy. She writes, "[T]he *female* mode—a style associative, nonhierarchical, persona, and open-ended. . . . Writers in this mode use language not to gain power but to create intimacy . . . intimacy often achieved through self-reflexive statements on the why and how of their practice. Such metadiscursive comments commonly announce the substitution of unconventional or multiple genres for the traditional essay, argue for personal over fixed forms" (3–4). Characteristics such as open-ended, self-reflexive, and personal are all applicable to the genre of the food blog, and we have seen the ways in which Wizenberg's and Ahern's blogs can be defined as such. In focusing on the private kitchen, these women bloggers share personal stories of their daily experiences with cooking. But their writing pushes back against more conventional genres with their blending of narrative styles. By transgressing narrative boundaries, these food blogs become an and/also rather than an either/or. In adopting this hybrid form, these writers use their structure to reinforce their themes—themes that call into question the binaries often supported by US American culture regarding perceptions of the space of the kitchen and women's preparation and consumption of food.

One formal element of food blogs that I have not yet discussed is the way in which these blogs enable women writers and readers to create an online community. In her book *The Discourse of Food Blogs: Multidisciplinary Perspectives* (2020), Daniela Cesiri reflects on the way in which these online blogs promote communication that, unlike the cookbook, is not "unidirectional" (2). She continues, "The genre of the blog is a very interesting and flexible form of computer-mediated communication (CMC) as it facilitates both asynchronous and synchronous communication in the recipes sections and in the comments sections, respectively" (2). Cesiri observes that—while cookbooks instruct an audience—the genre of the food blog enables the writer and the reader to communicate in significant ways. To me, this is one of the primary ways in which the food blog pushes back against the genre constraints of both the diary and the cookbook.

Both Wizenberg's and Ahern's early blog posts speak to this interactive nature. In the comments section of both women's blogs, you can see these exchanges that happen between author and reader. For instance, on 31 December 2005, kitchenMage writes: "This has left me inspired, and think I have sweet potatoes (not squash), walnut oil (not pumpkin), spinach (not wild greens), feta (not goat cheese), and lavendar [*sic*] salt (not lemon—although I must make some, your description made my mouth water!). Oddly enough, that all seems like I could swap it in and get some amusing variation." She concludes by writing, "I'll let you know how it goes." Ahern responds directly to this comment only several hours later, noting, "kitchen-Mage: Your variation sounds fabulous! Lavender salt? Wow. Let me know!" kitchenMage is a frequent commenter on Ahern's site, and she and Ahern often speak back to one another. Ahern references a suggestion of kitchenMage's in a blog post proper titled "Eating Vegan with Tomato-Fennel Soup." She writes, "Days earlier, I had made a spontaneous roasted vegetable stock, based on a suggestion that kitchenMage had left me in the comments section." This exchange is not singular to this reader. Rather, Ahern frequently references and responds to posts by readers, and those readers often write back as well.

Wizenberg also dialogues with her readers. In the comments that accompany her 31 August 2004 post, "Sir Bones: Is Stuffed,/De World, Wif Feeding Girls," she replies to two of the comments left by readers. Like Ahern, Wizenberg shows her appreciation of her followers by directly addressing the comments that they leave. In fact, Wizenberg and Ahern first became acquainted through reading one another's blogs. They write about time spent with each other. Wizenberg recalls an outing with Ahern at Mr. Spots Chai House in her post "Bigger and Fuller and Brighter" (22 Oct. 2007), and Ahern remembers making a soufflé with Wizenberg in a post titled "Souffle, Slowly, Sunday Afternoon, with Molly" (13 Oct. 2005). They frequently comment upon one another's posts as well. Their blogs, then, become "a distinct community-building space" (Presswood 44), which allows for "historically marginalized voices and alter the traditional canons of rhetoric, particular invention and arrangement" (Presswood 44).[11]

Ahern speaks directly to this power of connection in her 16 September 2005 post. In this post, she writes of the 1976 cookbook *Laurel's Kitchen: A Handbook of Vegetarian Cooking and Nutrition*, which was written by Laurel Robertson, Carol Flinders, and Bronwen Godfrey. One of the most powerful things about this text, Ahern notes, is the way in which its authors present a sense of community among themselves. She indicates in this post that her blog has enabled her to create her own community of women—women who love to cook and eat:

> And just like the women in *Laurel's Kitchen*, I finally have my community in the kitchen, people with whom I can swap recipes, talk politics, and share our lives. My dear friends in Seattle fill my kitchen frequently. But no longer limiting myself to the small world around me, I have this wonderfully funny and loving community of food bloggers around the world. We're the modern, global equivalent of church ladies putting together a cookbook for each other. And I would invite them into my humble little kitchen, any time.

Ahern and Wizenberg create for themselves a community of writers and readers who meditate on the ways in which their identities are informed by their relationships to kitchen space and the food they prepare and eat.

AFTERWORD

WRITER. EATER. COOK.

In the fall of 2009, the food magazine *Gourmet* unexpectedly folded. Writers covering the dissolution of the beloved publication expressed surprise. Writing for *Eater*, Amanda Klundt noted, "In a print media shocker today Media Decoder reports that Condé Nast is shutting down *Gourmet* magazine, the almost 70-year-old glossy food mag." Others, such as Stephanie Clifford writing for the *New York Times*, lauded the publication, noting, "*Gourmet* was to food what *Vogue* is to fashion, a magazine with a rich history and a perch high in the publishing firmament." Clifford sadly concluded that without *Gourmet*, "It's Rachel Ray's world now. We're all just cooking in it." No one, perhaps, was more surprised at the news than Ruth Reichl, the publication's editor-in-chief since 1999. As Reichl recalls in her memoir, *Save Me the Plums* (2019), after the announcement was made, the staff "looked at one another, uncomprehending. Close *Gourmet*? Surely we misunderstood. They could fire us all. Take the magazine in a new direction. But they could not shut down such a revered institution. A world without *Gourmet* was unimaginable" (249).

After *Gourmet*'s closing, Reichl struggled to make sense of her place in the food world. *Gourmet* was slated to release a cookbook, which included over 1,000 recipes, and feeling she owed it to the public, Reichl went on a book tour to promote the cookbook. It was also rumored that Reichl might write a memoir about her experiences at *Gourmet*. The food world waited. That memoir, however, did not come until ten years later. Instead, Reichl turned to her kitchen. She writes in the prologue to *My Kitchen Year: 136 Recipes That Saved My Life* (2015), "I had no idea what to do with the rest of my life and no notion of how we'd pay the bills. And so I did what I always do when I'm confused, lonely, or frightened: I disappeared into the kitchen" (xvi). Her "disappearance" resulted in two publications—*My Kitchen Year* and a novel titled *Delicious!* (2014).

Reichl is a food writer who spans the time period covered in *Season to Taste*. As noted earlier, born in 1948, Reichl's food-writing career began in 1972 with her cookbook *Mmmmm: A Feastiary*. Around the same time, she attained the position of food writer and editor for *New West* magazine. In the 1980s and early 1990s, she wrote for the *Los Angeles Times*, and then, in 1993, she became the restaurant critic for the *New York Times* before taking over *Gourmet* in 1999 ("Ruth Reichl: About"). During this time span, in addition to her magazine and newspaper writing, she produced four memoirs in addition to her 1972 cookbook. She continues to write today—both formally (with her published works) and also informally (on her blog and Twitter). On Twitter, Reichl has over 1.2 million followers, and, according to the title of Jason Diamond's piece for Literary Hub, she is "Redeeming the Twitter Hellscape One Tweet at a Time." Her prolific career, which spans decades, make Reichl's writing an excellent touchstone for changing attitudes about women and the space of the kitchen.

As we saw in chapter 2, Reichl was very much invested in presenting herself as a food-writing professional in her earlier work. While her first memoir, *Tender at the Bone* (1998), deals with home cooking, the text's most memorable chapter is a story of disastrous home cooking. In that chapter, Reichl recounts the time that her mother insisted on hosting a UNICEF fundraiser and engagement party;

Reichl's mother's food preparation was so poor that she accidentally gave all the guests food poisoning. In *Tender at the Bone*, Reichl stresses that "the most important thing in life is a good story" (x). This line, which comes in the book's opening chapter, immediately positions Reichl's text in the professional world of memoir writing. Reichl's second memoir, *Comfort Me with Apples* (2001), which I focused on in chapter 2, very much concentrates on the professional—rather than private—kitchen space. Reichl's 2005 memoir *Garlic and Sapphires* chronicles her time as the restaurant critic for the *New York Times*. The book is filled with stories about the lengths that she would go to conceal her identify from the restaurant she was reviewing. One of the most famous chapters, "Molly," is about the terrible experience she had while attending Le Cirque dressed as a middle-aged Midwesterner. When she returned later, as herself, she received much better treatment; *Garlic and Sapphires*, then, dealt in part with the discriminatory practices within the professional food world—a theme we also saw Reichl touch on in *Comfort Me with Apples*. It's interesting to note, too, that Reichl does not include a recipe list in either *Tender at the Bone* or *Comfort Me with Apples*—a move that can be read as another way of further distancing her writing from cookbooks and more directly aligning her work with the memoir.[1]

While Reichl embraces the professional sphere over the private sphere in her earlier works, her most recent publications focus more on the home kitchen. Reichl's shift in representation tracks with the changing attitudes we have seen in US American culture toward women and food. Like these contemporary food memoirists, Reichl takes a new approach to her relationship with food—the and/also rather than either/or approach, if you will. For instance, in her novel *Delicious!*, the young protagonist, Billie Breslin, initially abandons her home kitchen to pursue a job at a food magazine. Central to the plot, however, is Billie's need to return to the kitchen and overcome her fear of baking. While Billie was blessed with the gift of the perfect palate, her sister's untimely death and the emotional scars she carries from that incident have prevented her from embracing it. *Delicious!* charts Billie's attempts at healing herself from that tragedy and ultimately realizing that her place is, in fact, in the kitchen. Like many "second act" memoirs, the novel focuses on Billie's reinvention of herself, and central to that reinvention is the space of the kitchen.

My Kitchen Year finds Reichl herself rediscovering what that space means to her. The cookbook presents readers with 136 recipes that, according to the title, "saved" Reichl's life. In one chapter, she remembers sitting on a panel to celebrate *Gourmet* and being asked if she could have done anything differently to save the magazine. She ends the story with a visit to the farmers' market where she purchases some "large, watery, and not very flavorful" strawberries, which she uses to make "Roasted Winter Strawberries with Ice Cream" (105). She realizes at the close of this story that this dish served as "a fine reminder that no situation is ever hopeless" (105). Another story begins "I longed for the feel of a knife in my hand, the heft of water splashing into a pot. Yearned for the joyous sizzle, burble, and hiss that are the ever-changing soundtrack of the kitchen. I missed the daily transformations: fruit ripening, dough rising, bread toasting into golden slabs. I'd always thought of these elemental pleasures as minor diversions, but now I understood that they're the glue that holds me together" (225). These narratives and recipes focus on the home kitchen and the way in which that space is necessary to Reichl's healing from the trauma of *Gourmet* closing.

In her own "second act," Reichl began blogging and tweeting. Her first tweet appeared in January 2009. Her approach to Twitter has been described by Melanie Rehak of *Bookforum* as an "ongoing stream of Zen-like gustatory dispatches." In her feed, Reichl shares news about the food world (she commented on the death of Anthony Bourdain), photographs of food she has eaten, musings about life, and recipes for food she has cooked. Her Twitter account and the content she includes capture the new approach that she has taken in her food writing. On Twitter, her profile reads, "Writer.

Eater. Cook. Former Gourmet [*sic*] editor," establishing the various identities that she has now assumed.

Many of the recipes that she includes embrace these blurred lines between public and private, home cook and professional eater. For instance, in a tweet from 2 June 2018, she writes, "Sultry morning. And a perfect day for noodles." The recipe she links to in this tweet appears on her website under the "Ruth's Words" link—the section of her website where she blogs about food—a longer format than Twitter's 280 characters. In this linked post, "Gooey and Chewy," she starts by indicating that she had been reading food critic Jonathan Gold's article for the *Los Angeles Times* that relates his experiences at the Sichuan Summit, where he ate delicious food from L.A.'s best Sichuan restaurateurs. This article, Reichl writes, made her hungry for "Asian flavors," so she scours her pantry for ingredients. She ends up making—and sharing—her recipe for "Slightly Spicy Chinese Noodles with Squid," which she notes is based on celebrity Bruce Cost's recipe from his *Big Bowl Cookbook*. In this post, she does not distance herself from the food that she eats; instead, she shares her process for making this food, sharing photos, and including the recipe. She ends the post with her own tips to make this dish successful. At the same time, in this post, she reminds readers of her connections to the professional food world with her references to Gold and Cost.

In terms of content, this recipe blurs the lines between home kitchen/professional kitchen and private/public—from Reichl's indication that she adapted the recipe to her sharing of her techniques to her aligning the food she prepares with the work of a celebrity chef. And, in tweeting and blogging, Reichl exchanges the publication avenues that she has embraced in the past for more informal, personal writing—writing that is still public but that also enables her to connect with readers. Readers can directly engage with her writing by commenting on her blog posts and liking or even sharing her tweets.

Like the contemporary female food writers referenced throughout *Season to Taste*, Reichl's more recent work rejects the binary oppositions that were apparent in her earlier work. She explodes the divide of public/private in terms of her content and form, and she—like her contemporaries—complicates traditional perceptions of women, their relationship to food, and home cooking. Through the tangible act of preparing food, Reichl and her food-writing contemporaries encourage readers to reconsider the intangible politics of the kitchen.

NOTES

Introduction: Serve It Forth

1. A. O. Scott's review can be found in the 6 Aug. 2020 edition of the *New York Times*. Ramos reviews the film in her 5 Aug. 2009 blog post.

2. For a complete list of Child's television programming by year, see the Julia Child Foundation for Gastronomy and Culinary Arts. Additionally, you can find information about Julia's kitchen, featured on her television programs, on the Smithsonian's National Museum of American History website. As of this printing, the kitchen can be found on display at the National Museum of American History.

3. *The Best American Food Writing* (2018) served as the inaugural publication of Houghton Mifflin Harcourt's new Best American series. This series already includes such genres as essays, short stories, and sports writing.

4. *The Best American Food Writing* reflects this genre diversity by including essays previously published in periodicals as diverse as the *New Yorker, ESPN Magazine*, and *Eater*.

5. Reichl, when she was editor-in-chief at *Gourmet*, played a role in this elevation of chefs to celebrities when she featured such chefs as Laurent Gras, Suzanne Goin, Eric Ripert, Scott Conant, and Dean Fearing decked out as rock stars, complete with guitars and drums, on the Oct. 2003 restaurant edition of the magazine.

6. In Dec. 2020, *Variety* reported that the Food Network was one of the top twenty most watched networks on television, recording 952,000 viewers (Schneider). Comparatively, the top-viewed, most watched network at the time was CBS with 5,603,000 viewers (Schneider).

7. *Top Chef* premiered in 2006 and, as of this printing, has been in syndication for seventeen seasons.

8. For example, in 2008, Kohl's announced that Bobby Flay's product line would appear in stores ("Food Network and Kohl's Launch Bobby Flay-Branded Kitchenware and Casual Entertaining Products"), while in 2010 Target worked with Giada

128   Notes

De Laurentiis to develop a kitchenware line ("Target Launches Giada De Laurentiis for Target"). Rachael Ray, capitalizing on her popularity among Food Network fans, began a daytime television show in fall 2007 ("Rachael Ray Bio"). On her website, Rachaelray.com, you can buy a number of products—from cookware to olive oil (or EVOO in Ray-speak)—which Ray has developed.

9. The success of *Julie & Julia* paved the way for the subsequent summer release of *Eat Pray Love*—an adaptation of Elizabeth Gilbert's 2006 memoir of the same name that chronicles Gilbert's time in Italy, India, and Indonesia.

10. In his 2012 article "Seeds of Change: White House Kitchen Garden's Influence" for the *Washington Post* online, Tim Carman reported that there were more than 10,000 applications for school gardens to the National Gardening Association; 346 grants were available. He also notes, "There are 'people's gardens' in 'all 50 states, three U.S. territories and eight foreign countries,' according to the USDA, which launched the initiative in 2009, the same year as Michelle Obama's first kitchen garden planting."

11. In Washington, DC, where I live, one can find a variety of food trucks across the city. CapMac serves tomato soup in addition to their macaroni and cheese offerings, Red Hook Lobster provides lobster rolls, and Curbside Cupcakes has a variety of cupcakes for consumers to choose from. José Andrés's food truck, Pepe, boasts the 20-dollar *jamón íberico* sandwich referenced above (McKeever).

12. As early as 1796, with Amelia Simmons's *American Cookery*, US Americans became familiar with these instruction manuals for the kitchen, and in the years following, many more noteworthy cookbooks were shared with the public, including classics such as Eliza Acton's *Modern Cookery for Private Families* (1845), Isabella Beeton's *Mrs. Beeton's Book of Household Management*, and Fannie Farmer's *The Boston Cooking School Cookbook*. Today, many Americans are familiar with classic cookbooks such as *Betty Crocker's Cookbook* (1969) and *The Joy of Cooking* (1975) as well as cookbooks by celebrated chefs such as Edna Lewis, Julia Child, Alice Waters, and Martha Stewart.

13. Bittman was a *New York Times* columnist and writer. He has produced over twenty books, including the series of "how to cook everything" ("About Mark Bittman"). Colicchio is cofounder of the Gramercy Tavern in New York City and *Top Chef* cohost. In 2003, Colicchio opened 'Wichcraft, a sandwich shop devoted to providing customers with sustainable food ("Get to Know Our Story").

14. There are a few popular blogs worth mentioning specifically in order to illustrate the popularity of this genre. For instance, *Smitten Kitchen* (Deb Perelman) received thirty-nine reader comments on her 30 Jun. 2006 post "freedom, ringing," while on her 30 Jan. 2010 post for "best cocoa brownies" she received 1,152 comments from readers. On 25 Jan. 2007, the Homesick Texan's post "Cheese enchiladas: the essence of Tex-Mex" received 111. Both Perelman and Lisa Fain (Homesick Texan) won awards at *Saveur's* 1st Annual Food Blog Awards (2010)—Perelman for Best Individual Post and Best Food Photography and Fain for Best Regional Cuisine.

Notes   129

15. These numbers are from 1 Dec. 2021. Ruth Reichl is the food writer with the most books listed in the first ten entries; she has three on the list. Michael Pollan has two.

16. Hamilton owned the successful New York City restaurant Prune, which closed in 2020.

17. For example, as of 7 Jul. 2019, *101 Cookbooks'* Facebook page had 200,329 followers. At that time, Heidi J. Swanson, the site's creator, has 100,000 followers on Instagram.

18. Inness's collections include *Kitchen Culture in America: Popular Representations of Food, Gender, and Race* (2001), *Cooking Lessons: The Politics of Gender and Food* (2001), and *Pilaf, Pozole, and Pad Thai: American Women and Ethnic Food* (2001). For another disciplinary perspective on women and food, Kate Cairns and Josée Johnston published *Food and Femininity* (2015); in this qualitative study, which consists of interviews with over 100 food-oriented consumers, the authors explore the connections between food work (from shopping for food to preparing meals) and women and examine some of the controlling images, such as the nurturing mother and the diet-conscious working woman, that pervade popular culture.

19. For scholarly criticism of women's fiction and food, see Furst and Graham 1992; McGee 2001; Sceats 2000; and Heller and Moran 2003.

20. The 1980s produced extensive scholarly discussion of women's autobiographies. See, for example, Jelinek 1980; S. Smith 1987; and Benstock 1988. Theophano (2002) and Bower (1997) focus on the examination of cookbooks.

21. Hesser's text began as a column for the *New York Times*, and Julie Powell's book was adapted from her blog *The Julie/Julia Project*.

22. On the *Better Homes and Gardens* website, they note that the median income for their readers is $69,325 ("*Better Homes and Gardens*: Editorial Mission"), slightly above the national median income ($68,703) for US Americans reported in 2019 by the US Census Bureau (Semega et al.). They also report a ratio of eighty-one to nineteen female to male readers. There is no information included about race, but it can be assumed, in part because of the fairly homogenous racial representations of individuals within the pages of the magazine (white) and the fact that in the magazine industry publications that are not marketed toward primarily white people are clearly marked (e.g., *Jet, Essence*, and *Ebony*).

23. The third wave feminist movement is said to have begun in the mid-1990s. For more information on the third wave feminist movement, see R. Walker (1992) and Baumgardner and Richards (2000).

24. This term was developed by Tony Fry in *Design Futuring: Sustainability, Ethics, and New Practice* (2009).

25. Sunée was born in Korea and adopted and raised by a family from New Orleans, Louisiana. She spent time as a teenager traveling. The bulk of her narrative takes place in France although she visits other geographic locations.

26. Wizenberg has recently remarried and added Choi to her last name. I will refer to her as Wizenberg since that is the name under which she has published and I

am writing about her work prior to her marriage. At a point later in her career, Ahern titled her blog *Gluten-Free Girl and the Chef* to honor the work that she was doing with her husband, chef Danny Ahern. On 15 Feb. 2020, Ahern announced to readers that she would be taking her blog down, allowing access to it only by subscription.

27. The specific works that Belasco references here are Strasser's *Never Done: A History of American Housework* (1982); Schwartz Cowan's *More Work for Mother: The Ironies of Household Technology from the Open Hearth to the Microwave* (1983); Shapiro's *Perfection Salad: Women and Cooking at the Turn of the Century* (1986) and *Something from the Oven: Reinventing Dinner in 1950s America* (2005); DeVault's *Feeding the Family: The Social Organization of Caring as Gendered Work* (1991); Mennell et al.'s *The Sociology of Food: Eating, Diet, and Culture* (1992); and Avakian's *Through the Kitchen Window: Women Writers Explore the Intimate Meanings of Food and Cooking* (1997).

1. Design Challenge: *Better Homes and Gardens* and the Changing Space of the US American Kitchen

1. You can still purchase house plans through the *Better Homes and Gardens* website ("Find Your Dream House Plan"). There is even a search function that allows you to customize your square footage, number of bedrooms, number of bathrooms, stories, and garages. You can also select the style you are looking for as well as the type of collections (i.e., duplex, accessible, and pet lovers).

2. For a general introduction to architectural theory, see Mallgrave and Goodman (2011).

3. See Abel (2000).

4. For more information on identity and architecture, see Abel (2000) and Herrle and Wegerhoff (2008). Abel summarizes the connections between architecture and identity as such: "The importance of being able to interact in a personal way with architecture . . . in order to give proper expression to the personalities and social status of the occupants" (141). The essays included in Herrle and Wegerhoff are split into five categories: "The Making of Local Identity," "The Global and the Local," "Theoretical Concepts—Revisited," "Diversity as a Pattern of Local Architecture," and "Identities and 'Invented' Traditions"; each section takes a global approach to exploring identity. Included in this collection are such essays as Astrid Edlinger's "The Japanese Example—The Art of Appropriation," Mark R. O. Olweny and Jacqueline Wadulo's "Searching for Identity: Architecture and Urbanism in Uganda," and Styliane Philippou's "Nothing Is Foreign: Strategies of Brazilianisation of Modern Brazilian Architecture."

5. There are no page numbers in Colomina's introduction.

6. There have been scholars who have looked at personal identity politics and architecture from a variety of angles. For instance, Lesley Naa Norle Lokko's

Notes

131

collection *White Papers, Black Marks: Architecture, Race, and Culture* (2000) includes a variety of essays that focus on architecture and the politics of race. Likewise, Waldrep (2013) examines connections between identity politics and building, including chapters that focus on examining Native American identity and gay male identity in the analysis of the Foxwoods Casino and the architecture of Philip Johnson.

7. See, for example, Attfield and Kirkham (1989); Spain (1992); and Massey (1994).

8. Walker specifically mentions Susana Torre's *Women in American Architecture* (1977) and Dolores Hayden's *The Grand Domestic Revolution: Designs for American Homes, Neighborhoods, and Cities* (1982), noting that these were "among the earliest and most powerful" works (823).

9. Johnson notes some scholars who are an exception to her assertion, but she ultimately argues that critics often overlook the way in which identity politics, such as gender, informed home design (123).

10. It is important to note that both Plante and Cromley offer historical analyses of the architecture of the US American kitchen, primarily focusing on white women's changing roles and how these changes impacted the design of the US American kitchen. Both Plante and Cromley privilege the experiences of white women—be they domestics or matriarchs—in their analyses. Each allots only a few pages to addressing the way in which enslaved people might operate within the kitchen space. Deetz (2010) offers an excellent analysis of enslaved women's relationship to their kitchens, and her bibliography contains further reading on the topic. I also recommend Sharpless (2010), who offers insight into the role of Black domestic workers and their relationships to the kitchens they occupied.

11. While Reuss doesn't explicitly state that the magazine was primarily targeted at women or at white women, more specifically, it follows that women would have largely accounted for *Better Homes and Gardens'* readership given their historically close association with the home and the duties performed there. Today, *Better Homes and Gardens* includes detailed demographics of their readership on their webpage, noting that the magazine attracts primarily middle- to upper-class US American women ("*Better Homes and Gardens*: Editorial Mission"). Their self-reported demographic research does not include information about readership based on race; however, taking into account the racial representation on the pages of their magazine as well as the target audience for the advertisements included in the magazine, one can assume the readership is primarily white women.

12. According to the Pew Research Center, "Middle-income households—those with an income that is two-thirds to double the U.S. median household income—had incomes ranging from about $45,200 to $135,600 in 2016" (Bennett et al.).

13. These measurements are from the May, Oct., and Nov. issues, respectively.

14. For comparison, the size of an average bathroom in 2020 is around thirty-six to forty square feet. I searched a number of home renovations sites and most reported this figure.

132   Notes

15. There were only four issues in 1980 that did not feature kitchens in the table of contents—Jan., Jul., Sep., and Dec. The Jul. issue was dedicated to "100 Ideas under $100," and the Dec. issue featured primarily recipes and holiday crafts. The remaining two issues, which did not include kitchens in the table of contents—Jan. and Sep.—did, in fact, contain photographs of kitchens within the issue itself.

16. Architect Frank Lloyd Wright (1867–1959) was an early proponent of the open concept home; however, middle-class, US American homeowners did not embrace this design until later in the twentieth century. For more information, see Jacobs and Jacobs (1996).

17. I chose the Jan. and Sep. issues because the Jan. issue usually sets the tone for the year while the Sep. issue is usually one of the biggest issues.

18. The other remodel featured was for a master bedroom.

19. As noted earlier, women of different races and socioeconomic classes have always occupied the space of the kitchen; however, *Better Homes and Gardens* tends to represent primarily white, middle-class US American women on the pages of their magazine. In the earlier issues of the magazine that I examined, racial inclusion was limited. Even though men are now on the pages of *Better Homes and Gardens*, the majority of the figures represented on the pages are still white.

20. Two shots do not depict any individuals.

2. "A Woman's Most Rewarding Way of Life": The Feminist/ Housewife Debate and Contemporary Women's Response

1. The paperback edition of this book, which came out a year later, was retitled *For You Mom, Finally* (Sterling). Reportedly, Reichl never liked the original title and encouraged the publishers to change it for the paperback edition.

2. As a young girl, Reichl's mother, Miriam, resisted the expectations put upon women during that time period. She wanted to become a doctor but was told by her parents, "If you become a doctor no man will ever marry you" (8). Instead, she rebelled by receiving a PhD in musicology and then opening a bookstore where she corresponded with people like Christopher Morley and Max Eastman. Miriam eventually married and had a child, Robert; however, she divorced Robert's father, married again, and gave birth to Ruth.

3. The Matrix Awards ceremony, according to their website, is sponsored by New York Women in Communications, Inc. to honor "exceptional women from advertising, arts and entertainment, books, broadcasting, magazines, newspapers, public relations and new media." A video of Reichl's speech, given at the Hillside Club in Berkeley, California for the Berkeley Arts and Letters program, can be found at Fora.tv.

4. A handwritten copy of Tax's lyrics accompanied by illustrations can be found in the online collections of Duke University's Sallie Bingham Center for Women's

Notes 133

History and Culture. Tax explains on her personal website that as a member of the early feminist-socialist Boston-based group Bread and Roses, "When Bread and Roses started in 1969, I had a great burst of creativity and started putting new lyrics to old folk tunes. I even learned how to play the autoharp, though not very well. I have always believed that the most powerful and satisfying movements are ones that sing, and we certainly did." This particular song was to be sung to the tune of Alan Mills's "'There Was an Old Woman Who Swallowed a Fly.'"

5. Reichl mentions these dishes in the 8 Feb. 1987 article "A Departure for Alice's Restaurant," which can be found on the *Los Angeles Times*' website.

6. The article on McCarty was published in *New West* on 18 Jun. 1979, while the article about Chinese cuisine appeared in *Metropolitan Home* in May 1980.

3. Winking While We Bake: Recoding Kitchen Space in Contemporary Food Writing

1. The term "recoding" is from Fry, *Design Futuring*.

2. Both magazines continue to be published as of the printing of this book.

3. Groeneveld provides a plethora of examples of the way in which this distancing happens. She notes, "Beginning in the early 2000s, a spate of articles was published on the 'new knitting,' featuring titles such as 'Not Your Grandmother's Hobby' (Greider 2001); 'A Pastime of Grandma and the "Golden Girls" Evolves into a Hip New Hobby' (Lee 2005); 'Knitting: The New Yoga' (Marer 2002); 'Rock-and-Roll Knitters: They May Have Blue Hair, but They're No Grannies' (Scelfo 2004); and 'That Clicking Sound: Grandma's Favorite Hobby Hooks a New Generation of Young, Urban Go-Getters' (Tartakovsky 2000). As these titles demonstrate, the ways in which the resurgence of knitting was covered in the mainstream press emphasized the discourse of 'newness' and trendiness, frequently at the expense of grannies (the 'old knitters') who are constructed as the antithesis of cool, a demographic figured here more in terms of hip replacements than as just plain 'hip'" (127).

4. Matchar does not explicitly mention the race of the individuals that she interviewed for her study, nor does she reflect on the way in which racial politics play into this new domesticity.

5. Nina Bahadur discusses the uproar in her article "Female Chefs Respond to *Time* Magazine's 'Gods of Food,' Sexism in the Industry."

6. Melissa Weller, Petra Paradez, Kelly Fields, Ina Garten, and Michelle Polzine were all born and raised in America. Claire Saffitz was, too, though she was raised by an Ashkenazi Jewish family. Yossy Arefi has an Iranian father, Lara Lee has Indonesian roots, and Meera Sodha, who was on *The Guardian*'s list, also appears on this list. Hawa Hassan is of Somali heritage.

7. Previously, Diamond worked for Lancôme and Coach and was an editor at *Yahoo Food*, *Harper's Bazaar*, and *Women's Wear Daily* ("Kerry Diamond"). She

134   Notes

also co-owned the Smith Canteen coffee shop in Carroll Gardens ("Kerry Diamond"). Wu began her career for the magazines *Visionaire* and *V*, then worked at *Harper's Bazaar*, where she met her future *Cherry Bombe* partner, Kerry Diamond ("Claudia Wu"). Wu founded her own design firm, called Orphan, where she worked with Hugo Boss, NARS, Clinique, and Intermix, among others ("Claudia Wu"). She founded *Me* magazine, a publication dedicated to and guest edited by a different star for every issue ("Claudia Wu").

8. In addition to the magazine, the Cherry Bombe enterprise has a podcast, Cherry Bombe University (a weekend conference), and the *Cherry Bombe* Jubilee. At the 2018 Cherry Bombe University, there were sessions titled after fruits and topics that ranged from issues of food waste to setting a beautiful table. Past Jubilees have included speakers such as Joy Wilson of the blog *Joy the Baker* and food writer Madhur Jaffrey.

4. Kitchen Spaces: Sites of Resistance and Transformation

1. The series first aired in England on Channel 4.

2. Lawson's show became known for its nontraditional format; the show was filmed in her home kitchen and often contained shots of her busy family life.

3. Lawson's pedigree adds to this fascination; she is the daughter of Nigel Lawson, a former chancellor of the exchequer, and the late Vanessa Lawson, the heiress to the catering empire J. Lyons and Co. Lawson was married to fellow journalist John Diamond, who died tragically in 2001 at the age of forty-seven, leaving Lawson a widow and the caretaker of two small children ("Nigella Lawson").

4. Feminist film scholar Laura Mulvey coined this term in her 1973 essay "Visual Pleasure and Narrative Cinema," where she outlines the ways in which women become the passive object of the active male gaze in film.

5. In "The Eight Sexiest Women on TV Cooking Shows," Giada is shown in a bikini (Ost). The accompanying text reads, "Giada is Italian-born, low-cut T-shirt-wearing, and a bit lollipoplike, but we wouldn't mind finding out how many licks it takes to get to the center of *her* Tootsie Pop. Her tiny frame supports a head with perfect skin and a smile so bright it seems to have the power to conjure birds and butterflies to help her cook a meal. Perfect doll Giada is a Disney princess come to life" (Ost). In fact, of the eight women featured, only one is shown in professional attire (an apron). The other photographs are closeup shots of the women's faces or a full body shot as with Lawson's photograph. One (that of Nadia G. of *Bitchin Kitchen*) is a grainy image of Nadia wearing fur and leopard and bright red lipstick with what appears to be a bed in the background. By contrast, the men featured in *People's* "These Are the Sexiest Male Chefs in America 2017" are not as sexualized (Spence). The first photograph of the Cooking Channel's Jordan Andino shows

Andino shirtless, but that photograph is an anomaly. Most of the other chefs are pictured in professional attire—whether it be chefs' coats or suits and ties.

6. In this paragraph, I am only listing a few of the most well known of those scholars who write about women, the body, food, and sex. There are many excellent works that explore these topics individually or in connection with one another.

7. Kilbourne cowrote *So Sexy So Soon: The New Sexualized Childhood and What Parents Can Do to Protect Their Kids* (2008) with Diane E. Levin.

8. Jovanovski's reading of Lawson and her work is in opposition to my previous reading of Lawson. In her analysis of Lawson, Jovanovski notes that one of the issues with Lawson's hedonistic food femininity is that while she professes to enjoy food—and demonstrates her love of food through the act of eating—her cookbooks and interviews are often peppered with body-policing language. As a result, Jovanovski argues, "[Nigella] is implicitly reinforcing a narrative of normative discontent that is already pervasive in mainstream Western culture. Rather than resisting this message, she subtly normalizes it by casually referencing it in her language." Joanne Hollows in her essay "Feeling Like a Domestic Goddess: Postfeminism and Cooking" (2003) creates a compelling argument as to why Lawson is an emancipatory figure, highlighting the ways in which women can enjoy food and delight in the pleasure and nourishment that come with that food. I am in agreement with Hollows's reading of Lawson.

9. You can find Powell's blog posts at *What Could Happen?*

10. For more information on this subgenre that Kimberly D. Nettles-Barcelón labels "second acts," see her article "Women and Entrepreneurial Food-Work: Second Acts, 'New Domesticity,' and the Continuing Significance of Racialized Difference" (2017).

11. After their relationship is consummated, Melucci shares her recipe for "Morning After Pumpkin Bread."

12. Melucci does not deal with these five men exclusively; she also references, more briefly, other relationships.

13. There are only a few exceptions. There are recipes included in her chapter "Single-Girl Suppers" not attributed to anyone as well as a few recipes of Lachlan's.

14. Baussan is the founder of L'Occitane en Provence—a high-end beauty and home goods franchise.

15. I first encountered the term "docility myth" in an article written by Christine Ro for BBC online; however, additional scholarship that explores the behavior myths associated with Asians is plentiful. Rosaline S. Chou and Joe Feagin's *Myth of the Model Minority: Asian Americans Facing Racism* (2015) is a more recent work that explores stereotypes of Asian Americans. The term "model minority" was first coined in 1966 by sociologist William Peterson in an article for the *New York Times* titled "Success Story: Japanese American Style."

16. It is not surprising that Sunée's misery manifests itself in failure to eat. As scholars of anorexia nervosa and bulimia have noted, these diseases are a way

for people to exhibit control over their bodies in the face of sometimes chaotic outside influences.

17. In "Le Repas Maigre," Sunée writes of attempting to cook Christmas dinner but eventually allowing Olivier to take charge because she cannot complete the task. In "Some Enchanted Life," she cooks a meal in Olivier's Paris apartment before throwing it all in the trash.

18. According to Hawbaker's website, their preferred pronouns are "they/their."

19. Hawbaker acknowledges the tricky pleasure politics of Lawson, especially because of the reaction of heterosexual men to the domestic goddess. But they determine that Lawson's messages regarding love and appreciation of the self ultimately cancels out the male gaze.

5. The Gender Politics of Meat: The Foodie Romance and Julie Powell's *Cleaving*

1. Throughout her memoir, Powell refers to her lover only as D. She does not include a period after the initial.

2. There are two women in this space: Hailey, who works at the shop, and Jessica, who is wife to and part owner of the shop. However, Powell devotes much less narrative time to these two women.

3. In her book, Cooper indicates that, as of the writing of her book, only one woman in the world—Lyde Buchtenkirch-Biscardi—had obtained the title of Certified Master Chef (25). Since the publication of Cooper's book, no other women have been awarded the Certified Master Chef title. Lynne Gigliotti, a Chef Instructor/Associate Professor at the Culinary Institute of America who appeared on *Top Chef: Season 7*, was said to have been pursuing it, but when I contacted her via email in 2012, she confirmed that neither she nor any other woman has received the title.

4. ROC-United includes their rationale for focusing on California, "By focusing on the state with the largest restaurant industry, California, which includes several cities that are repeatedly named among the top dining destinations nationwide and one of the most diverse populations of any state in the country, the findings in this report have national significance" (Restaurant Opportunities Centers United, "Ending Jim Crow"). In terms of how they conducted the study, they explain, "Based on government data analysis, a limited pool of employer interviews, and interviews with experts, the initial findings explored in this report suggest the need for further research to more deeply understand the restaurant industry's occupational segregation problem and how to address it" (Restaurant Opportunities Centers United, "Ending Jim Crow").

5. For more information on these incidents, see Maynard (2017).

6. In his article, Rocheleau relies on statistics from the US Department of Labor.

7. On October 26, 2022, Julie Powell, age forty-nine, passed away from cardiac arrest.

Notes

8. This scene becomes even more confusing when the narrative immediately shifts to a present-day Camille masturbating, confusing the violence of the shed with titillation. There are also many moments in *Sharp Objects* when women and pigs are conflated. One of the main characters, Amma, lives close to a pig farm and visits. The dead girls that are discovered have had their teeth removed, and in order to test the probability of a woman committing the crime the detective assigned to the case attempts to remove the teeth from a dead pig.

9. This moment becomes more problematic, when it is implied that Camille was raped in this area of the woods.

6. Blog Her: Transgressing Narrative Boundaries

1. For more information on BlogHer's beginnings, see Mousumi Saha Kumar's article for BrainPrick.

2. I corresponded via email with Wu in Aug. 2012.

3. In our email exchange, Wu reported that the 2012 conference had 5,100 registered attendees. In 2011, it was 4,000+ attendees. She also noted that only 5 percent of the attendees in 2012 were men.

4. The first "subconference" was for business blogging.

5. Presswood notes that his percentage comes from a study published by *Graphic Sociology* in 2012.

6. The categories included "Best Baking and Desserts Blog," "Best Wine Blog," "Best Food Photography," "Best Regional Cuisine," "Best Special Interest Blog," "Best Culinary Travel," "Best Individual Post," "Most Innovative Video Content," and "Best Kitchen Tools and Hardware Coverage." Deb Perelman, of *Smitten Kitchen*, won for both "Best Individual Post" and "Best Food Photography."

7. The Bloggies were the largest and longest running blog awards. The creator, Nikolai Nolon, ended the awards in 2015.

8. The winners of these awards were *Cooking for Engineers* (2005), *Vegan Lunch Box* (2006), *Help! I Have a Fire in My Kitchen* (2007), *The Pioneer Woman Cooks* (2008, 2011, and 2013), *Cake Wrecks* (2009), *Bakerella* (2010), and *Smitten Kitchen* (2012, 2014, and 2015). *Cooking for Engineers* and *Help! I Have a Fire in My Kitchen* are authored by men; *Cake Wrecks* is a collaborative blog.

9. There has been some excellent scholarship on blogging, including Serfaty's work. For more information on blogging in general, see such works as David Hudson's *Blogging* (2011), Qi Wang's *The Autobiographical Self in Time and Culture* (2013), and Jill Walker Rettberg's *Blogging* (2014). In addition to Presswood and Cesiri, Tisha Dejmanee's 2016 "'Food as Porn' as Postfeminist Play: Digital Femininity and the Female Body on Food Blogs" for *Television and New Media* as well as Alexandra Rodney, Sarah Cappeliez, Merin Oleschuk, and Josée Johnston's 2017 article for *Food, Culture, and Society* offer an excellent analysis of women's food blogs.

10. For more information on the topic of blogs and genre, see Miller and Shepherd (2009).

11. Presswood's chapter "Constitutive Rhetoric and Digital Communities" is particularly pertinent to this discussion.

Afterword: Writer. Eater. Cook.

1. *Garlic and Sapphires* does contain a "Recipe Index," but it only lists the various dishes from the memoir proper. It does not even provide a page number for the reader to cross-reference those recipes.

BIBLIOGRAPHY

"#WeAreSHE." She Media, https://www.shemedia.com/about. Accessed 21 Jan. 2021.

@cookbook. "Chocolate Rosemary Tart: warm c crm/1/8t salt/sprgrosemry15m@ low. Strain, +12oz choc. Offheat+2yolk/egg/1/4c sug. Fill crumbcrust.30m@325F." *Twitter*, 25 Nov. 2018, https://twitter.com/cookbook/status/1066570562858668032.

@ruthreichl. "Sultry morning. And a perfect day for noodles: ruthreichl.com /ruth-words." *Twitter*, 2 Jun. 2018, 10:56 am, https://twitter.com/ruthreichl /status/1002926842041589762/.

Abel, Chris. *Architecture and Identity: Responses to Cultural and Technological Change*. Architectural Press, 2000.

"About *BUST*." *BUST*, https://bust.com/info/about-info-menu-47.html. Accessed 21 Dec. 2020.

"About Goodreads." *Goodreads*, https://www.goodreads.com/about/us. Accessed 10 Jan. 2022.

"About Mark Bittman." *How to Cook Everything*, http://www.howtocookevery thing.com/about-mark-bittman. Accessed 15 Dec. 2020.

"About Us." *BlogHer*, https://www.blogher.com/about. Accessed 21 Jan. 2021.

"About Us." *Restaurant Opportunities Centers United*, https://rocunited.org/. Accessed 16 Sep. 2019.

Adams, Carol. *The Pornography of Meat*. Continuum, 2003.

Adams, Carol. *The Sexual Politics of Meat*. Continuum, 1990.

Ahern, Shauna James. *Enough: Notes from a Woman Who Has Finally Found It*. Sasquatch, 2020.

Ahern, Shauna James. *Gluten-Free Girl: How I Found the Food That Loves Me Back and How You Can Too*. Wiley, 2009.

Ahern, Shauna James. *Gluten-Free Girl*, https://www.glutenfreegirl.blogspot.com. Accessed 10 Jan. 2020.

Ahern, Shauna James, and Daniel Ahern. *Gluten-Free Girl American Classics Reinvented*. Houghton Mifflin Harcourt, 2015.

Bibliography

Ahern, Shauna James, and Daniel Ahern. *Gluten-Free Girl and the Chef: A Love Story with 100 Tempting Recipes.* Wiley, 2012.

Ahern, Shauna James, and Daniel Ahern. *Gluten-Free Girl Every Day.* Houghton Mifflin Harcourt, 2013.

Allen, Thomas W. Comment on *Cleaving: A Story of Marriage, Meat, and Obsession." Amazon,* 29 Nov. 2009, https://www.amazon.com/Cleaving-Story -Marriage-Meat-Obsession/dp/B005IV17EO.

Attfield, Judy, and Pat Kirkham. *A View from the Interior: Women and Design.* The Women's Press, 1989.

Avakian, Arlene. "Cooking Up Lives: Feminist Food Memoirs." *Feminist Studies,* vol. 42, no. 2, 2014, pp. 277–303. *JSTOR,* https://www.jstor.org/stable/10.15767 /feministstudies.40.2.277. Accessed 12 Jan. 2022.

Avakian, Arlene. *Through the Kitchen Window: Women Explore the Intimate Meaning of Food and Cooking.* Beacon, 1997.

Avakian, Arlene, and Barbara Haber, editors. *From Betty Crocker to Feminist Food Studies: Critical Perspectives on Women and Food.* University of Massachusetts Press, 2005.

Bahadur, Nina. "Female Chefs Respond to Time Magazine's 'Gods of Food,' Sexism in the Industry." *Huffington Post,* 14 Nov. 2013, https://www.huffpost.com/entry /female-chefs-respond-time-gods-of-food_n_4273610. Accessed 15 Jan. 2022.

"Barbara Kruger." *Mary Boone Gallery,* https://www.maryboonegallery.com/artist /barbara-kruger. Accessed 18 Dec. 2020.

"Barbara Kruger: *Untitled (Connect)." Phillips,* https://www.phillips.com/detail /barbara-kruger/NY011018/19/. Accessed 18 Dec. 2020.

Barclay, Eliza. "Bloggers Replace Mom's Recipe Box as Source of Food Knowledge." *NPR's The Salt,* 2 Mar. 2010, https://www.npr.org/sections /thesalt/2012/03/02/147809819/bloggers-replace-moms-recipe-box-as-source -of-food-knowledge.

Basker, Gideon, Karen Brooks, Leland Payton, and Crystal Payton, with Lisa Hall. *Patio Daddy-o: '50s Recipes with a Modern Twist.* Chronicle, 1996.

Baumgardner, Jennifer, and Amy Richards. *Manifesta: Young Women, Feminism, and the Future.* Farrar, Straus, and Giroux, 2000.

Beck, Simone, Louisette Bertholle, and Julia Child. *Mastering the Art of French Cooking.* Knopf, 1961.

Belasco, Warren. *Food: The Key Concepts.* Berg, 2008.

Bennett, Jesse, Richard Fry, and Rakesh Kochhar. "Are You in the American Middle Class? Find Out with Our Income Calculator." *Pew Research Center,* 23 Jul. 2020, https://www.pewresearch.org/fact-tank/2020/07/23/are-you-in -the-american-middle-class/.

Benstock, Shari, editor. *The Private Self: Theory and Practice of Women's Autobiographical Writings.* University of North Carolina Press, 1988.

Berke, Richard L. "The 1992 Campaign: Democrats; Brown and Clinton Shout It Out in a Debate." *New York Times,* 16 Mar. 1992, https://www.nytimes.com

Bibliography 141

/1992/03/16/us/the-1992-campaign-democrats-brown-and-clinton-shout-it
-out-in-a-debate.html.

Better Homes and Gardens. Jan.–Dec. 1960.

Better Homes and Gardens. Jan.–Dec. 1970.

Better Homes and Gardens. Jan.–Dec. 1980.

Better Homes and Gardens. Jan.–Dec. 1990.

Better Homes and Gardens. Jan.–Dec. 2000.

Better Homes and Gardens. Jan.–Dec. 2010.

"*Better Homes and Gardens Magazine.*" *Better Homes and Gardens*, https://www
.bhg.com/better-homes-and-garden-magazine/. Accessed 30 Jan. 2021.

"*Better Homes and Gardens*: Editorial Mission." *Meredith Direct Media*, https://mer-
edithdirectmedia.com/magazines/better-homes-gardens. Accessed 15 Dec. 2020.

Bitch. Winter 2004.

Bitch. Winter 2005.

"BlogHer Co-founders Lisa Stone, Elisa Camahort Page, and Jory Des Jardins
Among FORTUNE's 2013 Most Powerful Women Entrepreneurs." *PRWeb*, 13
Sep. 2013, https://www.prweb.com/releases/blogher_fortunes/most_powerful
_women/prweb11112205.htm.

"BlogHer Network Joins Ranks of Top Women's Networks Online." *Media Report
to Women*, vol. 35, no. 4, fall 2007, pp. 1–3. *Academic Search Complete*, http://
search.ebscohost.com/login.aspx?direct+true&da=a9h&AN+27588194&site=
ehost-live. Accessed 22 Jan. 2021.

Bloom, Lynn Z. "Consuming Prose: The Delectable Rhetoric of Food Writing."
College English, vol. 70, no. 4, Mar. 2008, pp. 346–62. *MLA International
Bibliography*, http://proxygw.wrlc.org/login?url=https://search.ebscohost.
com/login.aspx?direct=true&db=mzh&AN=2008300260&site=ehost-live.
Accessed 15 Dec. 2020.

Bloom, Lynn Z. "Feminist Culinary Autobiography: *Batterie de Cuisine* to Peace-
able Kingdom." *Food, Feminisms, Rhetorics*, edited by Melissa A. Goldthwaite.
Southern Illinois University, 2017, pp. 89–99.

Bollen, Christopher. "Barbara Kruger." Interview, 13 Feb. 2013, https://www.inter
viewmagazine.com/art/barbara-kruger.

Bordo, Susan. *Unbearable Weight: Feminism, Western Culture, and the Body*.
University of California Press, 1993.

Bower, Anne. *Recipes for Reading: Community Cookbooks, Stories, and Histories*.
University of Massachusetts Press, 1997.

Bracken, Peg. *The I Hate to Cook Book*. 1960. Grand Central Publishing, 2010.

"Brown Takes Second Place in Michigan." *Facts on File World Digest*, 19 Mar.
1992. *Nexis-Uni*, https://advance-lexis-com.proxygw.wrlc.org/api/document?c
ollection=news&id=urn:contentItem:3SJ4-GBB0-000Y-N4M4-00000
-00&context=1516831. Accessed 12 Jan. 2022.

Brownley, Martine Watson, and Allison B. Kimmich, editors. *Women and
Autobiography*. SR Books, 1999.

Buch, Clarissa. "Why the James Beard Foundation Is Fostering Today's Female Chefs." *The Observer*, 21 Mar. 2018, https://observer.com/2018/03/james-beard-foundation-gender-inequality-in-restaurant-industry/.

Bullock-Prado, Gesine, and Raymond G. Prado. *My Life from Scratch: A Sweet Journey of Starting Over, One Cake at a Time*. Broadway Books, 2009.

BUST. Spring 2004.

"Butchers and Other Meat, Poultry, and Fish Processing Workers." *Data USA*, https://datausa.io/profile/soc/butchers-other-meat-poultry-fish-processing-workers. Accessed 4 Jan. 2021.

Cairns, Kate, and Josée Johnston. *Food and Femininity*. Bloomsbury, 2015.

Carman, Tim. "Seeds of Change: White House Kitchen Garden's Influence." *Washington Post*, 26 Mar. 2012, https://www.washingtonpost.com/.

Carrie. Comment on "*Cleaving: A Story of Marriage, Meat, and Obsession*." *Amazon*, 16 Apr. 2015, https://www.amazon.com/Cleaving-Story-Marriage-Meat-Obsession/dp/B005IV17EO.

Cesiri, Daniela. *The Discourse of Food Blogs: Multidisciplinary Perspectives*. Routledge, 2020.

"Chef: Molly Wizenberg." *The James Beard Foundation*, https://www.jamesbeard.org/chef/molly-wizenberg. Accessed 23 Jan. 2021.

Cherry Bombe. Spring/Summer 2014.

Cherry Bombe. Fall/Winter 2014.

Cherry Bombe. Fall/Winter 2015.

Cherry Bombe. Spring/Summer 2017.

Cherry Bombe. Spring/Summer 2020.

Chou, Rosaline S., and Joe Feagin. *Myth of the Model Minority: Asian Americans Facing Racism*. Paradigm Publishers, 2015.

Christel S. Hachigian. Comment on "*Cleaving: A Story of Marriage, Meat, and Obsession*." *Amazon*, 22 Dec. 2009, https://www.amazon.com/Cleaving-Story-Marriage-Meat-Obsession/dp/B005IV17EO.

Chua-Eoan, Howard. "The 13 Gods of Food." *Time*, 7 Nov. 2013, https://time100.time.com/2013/11/07/the-13-gods-of-food/.

"Claudia Wu." *Wikipedia*, https://en.wikipedia.org/wiki/Claudia_Wu. Accessed 21 Dec. 2020.

Cleaving: A Story of Marriage, Meat, and Obsession. *Amazon*, https://www.amazon.com/Cleaving-Story-Marriage-Meat-Obsession/dp/B005IV17EO. Accessed 16 Sep. 2019.

Clifford, Stephanie. "Condé Nast Closes *Gourmet* and Three Other Magazines." *New York Times*, 5 Oct. 2009, https://www.nytimes.com/2009/10/06/business/media/06gourmet.html.

Colomina, Beatriz, editor. *Sexuality and Space*. Princeton Papers on Architecture, 1992.

Coontz, Stephanie. *The Way We Never Were: American Families and the Nostalgia Trap*. Basic, 1992.

Bibliography

Cooper, Ann. *A Woman's Place Is in the Kitchen: The Evolution of Women Chefs.* Wiley, 1997.

Cooper, Gael L. *Service Is the Secret: E. T. Meredith's Search for Service Journalism.* 1988. University of Missouri-Columbia, Master's Thesis.

Corliss, Richard. "Box-Office Weekend: G.I. Just O.K., Julia Delicious." *Time*, 10 Aug. 2009, http://content.time.com/time/arts/article/0,8599,1915441,00.html.

Cortina, Melissa. "Yes, I Am a 'Female Butcher:' And My Gender Has Nothing to Do with It." *The New Food Economy*, 17 Aug. 2017, https://newfoodeconomy .org/yes-i-am-a-female-butcher/.

Counihan, Carole, and Penny Van Esterik, editors. *Food and Culture: A Reader.* 3rd ed. Routledge, 2013.

Cromley, Elizabeth Collins. *The Food Axis: Cooking, Eating, and the Architecture of American Houses.* University of Virginia Press, 2010.

"Crusty, Herb-Fried Chicken." *Better Homes and Gardens*, https://www.bhg.com /recipe/crusty-herb-fried-chicken/. Accessed 17 Dec. 2020.

Deck, Alice A. "Now Then—Who Said Biscuits? The Black Woman Cook as Fetish in American Advertising, 1905–1953." *Kitchen Culture in America: Popular Representations of Food, Gender, and Race*, edited by Sherrie A. Inness, University of Pennsylvania, 2001, pp. 69–93.

Deetz, Kelley. 'When Her Thousand Chimneys Smoked': *Virginia's Enslaved Cooks and Their Kitchen.* 2010. University of California, Berkeley, PhD Dissertation.

Dejmanee, Tisha. "'Food Porn' as Postfeminist Play: Digital Femininity and the Female Body on Food Blogs." *Television and New Media*, vol. 17, no. 5, 2016, pp. 429–48. *SAGE Journals*, https:/doi.org/10.1177/1527476415615944.

Delk Adams, Jocelyn. *Grandbaby Cakes: Modern Recipes, Vintage Charm, Soulful Memories.* Surrey Books, 2015.

Delk Adams, Jocelyn. *Grandbaby Cakes*, https://grandbaby-cakes.com/. Accessed 20 Dec. 2020.

DeVault, Marjorie L. *Feeding the Family: The Social Organization of Caring as Gendered Work.* University of Chicago Press, 1991.

Diamond, Jason. "Redeeming the Twitter Hellscape One Tweet at a Time." *Literary Hub*, 11 Apr. 2019, https://lithub.com/ruth-reichl-redeeming-the -twitter-hellscape-one-tweet-at-a-time/.

Duff, David. *Modern Genre Theory.* Longman, 2000.

Eagleton, Mary. "Gender and Genre." *Re-Reading the Short Story*, edited by Clare Hansen, St. Martin's, 1998, pp. 55–68.

Elvin, John. "Pork 'n' Poke." *Washington Times*, 19 Mar. 1992. *NewsBank*, https:// infoweb.newsbank.com/apps/news/document-view?p=WORLDNEWS&docr ef=news/0EB0EF8A88647BC6&f=basic. Accessed 12 Jan. 2022.

Ephron, Nora, director. *Julie & Julia.* Sony Pictures, 2009.

Erway, Cathy. *The Art of Eating In: How I Learned to Stop Spending and Love the Stove.* Gotham Books, 2010.

Fain, Lisa. "Cheese enchiladas: the essence of Tex-Mex." *Homesick Texan*, 25 Jan. 2007, https://www.homesicktexan.com/2021/02/essence-of-tex-mex.html.

Favilli, Elena. "Julia Child." *Good Night Stories for Rebel Girls*. Harper Collins, 2016.

Felton, Lena. "Alison Roman's Comments about Chrissy Teigen and Marie Kondo Lit a Fire. Here's Why It's Still Burning." *The Lily*, 11 May 2020, https://www.thelily.com/alison-romans-comments-about-chrissy-teigen-and-marie-kondo-lit-a-fire-heres-why-its-still-burning/.

"Find Your Dream House Plan." *Better Homes and Gardens*, https://houseplans.bhg.com/. Accessed 17 Dec. 2020.

Flinn, Kathleen. *The Sharper Your Knife, The Less You Cry: Love, Learning, and Tears at the World's Most Famous Cookery School*. Portrait, 2008.

"Food Network and Kohl's Launch Bobby Flay-Branded Kitchenware and Casual Entertaining Products." *Food Network*, 15 May 2008, https://corporate.kohls.com/content/dam/kohlscorp/pdfs/2008/BFKohl'sInstore.pdf.

Freedman, Diane P. *An Alchemy of Genres: Cross-Genre Writing by American Feminist Poet-Critics*. University Press of Virginia, 1992.

Friedan, Betty. *The Feminine Mystique*. 1963, Norton, 2001.

Fry, Tony. *Design Futuring: Sustainability, Ethics, and New Practice*. Bloomsbury, 2009.

Furst, Lilian R., and Peter W. Graham, editors. *Disorderly Eaters: Texts in Self-Empowerment*. Pennsylvania State University Press, 1992.

Gamez, Isao. "Rachael Ray's Job in Job in Jeopardy over Massive Weight Gain? The Food Guru Is Eating Herself Out of a Career!" *Radar Online*, 7 Feb. 2017, https://radaronline.com/photos/rachael-ray-fat-weight-gain-photo-too-fat-tv-star-food-network/.

"Get To Know Our Story." *'Wichcraft*, https://www.wichcraft.com/about/. Accessed 15 Dec. 2020.

Gigliotti, Lynne. "Re: Research Question—Book Publication." Received by Caroline Smith, 5 Jun. 2012.

Gillis, Stacy, and Joanne Hollows. *Feminism, Domesticity, and Popular Culture*. Routledge, 2009.

Goeller, Alison D. "The Hungry Self: The Politics of Food in Italian American Women's Autobiography." *Prose Studies: History, Theory, Criticism*, vol. 27, no. 3, Dec. 2005, pp. 235–47, https://doi.org/10.1080/01440350500223818.

Gordon, Megan. "Could Online Recipes Really Replace Mom's Recipe Box?" *theKitchn*, 8 Mar. 2012, https://www.thekitchn.com/could-online-recipes-really-replace-moms-recipe-box-167109.

"Green Chile Fried Chicken." *Better Homes and Gardens*, https://www.bhg.com/recipe/green-chile-fried-chicken/. Accessed 17 Dec. 2020.

Groeneveld, Elizabeth. *Making Feminist Media: Third-Wave Magazines on the Cusp of the Digital Age*. Wilfrid Laurier Press, 2016.

Bibliography

Guignery, Vanessa. "Hybridity, Why It Still Matters." *Hybridity: Forms and Figures in Literature and the Visual Arts*, edited by Vanessa Guignery, Catherine Pessi-Miquel, and François Specq, Cambridge Scholars, 2011, pp. 1–8.

Halloran, Vivian Nun. *The Immigrant Kitchen: Food, Ethnicity, and Diaspora.* Ohio State University Press, 2016.

Hansen Shaevitz, Marjorie. *The Superwoman Syndrome.* Warner Books, 1984.

Hawbaker, K. T. "How Nigella Lawson and Ina Garten Helped Me Love My Fat, Queer Self." *Bon Appetit*, 3 Jun. 2019, https://www.bonappetit.com/story/nigella-lawson-ina-garten.

Hayden, Dolores. *The Grand Domestic Revolution: Designs for American Homes, Neighborhoods, and Cities.* MIT Press, 1982.

HBS Dealer Staff. "Houzz Chronicles the Emergence of the Super Kitchen." *HBS Dealer*, 20 Feb. 2020, https://www.hbsdealer.com/news/houzz-chronicles-emergence-super-kitchen.

Heart of Dinner. https://www.heartofdinner.com/. Accessed 21 Dec. 2020.

Heller, Tamar, and Patricia Moran, editors. *Scenes of the Apple: Food and the Female Body in Nineteenth-and-Twentieth-Century Women's Writing.* State University of New York Press, 2003.

Herrle, Peter, and Erik Wegerhoff. *Architecture and Identity.* Lit, 2008.

Hirschberg, Lynne. "Hot Dish." *New York Times Magazine*, 18 Nov. 2001, https://www.nytimes.com/2001/11/18/magazine/hot-dish.html.

Hollows, Joanne. *Domestic Cultures.* Open University Press, 2008.

Hollows, Joanne. "Feeling Like a Domestic Goddess: Postfeminism and Cooking." *European Journal of Cultural Studies*, vol. 6, no. 2, 1 May 2003, pp. 179–202. *SAGE Journals*, https:/doi.org/10.1177/1367549403006002003.

Holmes, Linda. "What's Wrong with Julie Powell's 'Cleaving.'" *Pop Culture Happy Hour*, NPR, 10 Dec. 2009, https://www.npr.org/2009/12/10/114431078/whats-wrong-with-julie-powells-cleaving.

Hudson, David L. *Blogging.* Chelsea House, 2011.

Inge, Leoneda. "Female Butchers Are Slicing Through the Meat World's Glass Ceiling." *The Salt.* NPR, 7 Dec. 2014, https://www.npr.org/sections/thesalt/2014/12/07/366642071/women-butchers-are-slicing-through-the-meat-worlds-glass-ceiling.

Inness, Sherrie, editor. *Cooking Lessons: The Politics of Gender and Food.* Rowman & Littlefield, 2001.

Inness, Sherrie. *Dinner Roles: American Women and Culinary Culture.* University of Iowa City, 2001.

Inness, Sherrie, editor. *Kitchen Culture in America: Popular Representations of Food, Gender, and Race.* University of Pennsylvania Press, 2001.

Inness, Sherrie, editor. *Pilaf, Pozole, and Pad Thai: American Women and Ethnic Food.* University of Massachusetts Press, 2001.

Inness, Sherrie. *Secret Ingredients: Race, Class, and Gender at the Dinner Table*. Palgrave Macmillan, 2006.

Jackson, Kate. "Why Are People Obsessed with the Size of Female Chefs? No One Ever Calls Gordon Ramsay Fat." *The Sun*, 6 Apr. 2016, https://www.thesun.co.uk/archives/news/1047099/why-are-people-obsessed-with-the-size-of-female-chefs-no-one-ever-calls-gordon-ramsay-fat/.

Jacobs, Herbert, and Katherine Jacobs. *Building with Frank Lloyd Wright: An Illustrated Memoir*. Southern Illinois Press, 1996.

Jaworski, Margaret. "Circle This: Bi-Partisan Bake Off." *Family Circle*, 21 Jul. 1992, p. 9.

Jelinek, Estelle, editor. *Women's Autobiography: Essays in Criticism*. Indiana University Press, 1980.

"Jocelyn and Joyce: Around My Table, Presented by Classico." *Food Network*, https://www.foodnetwork.com/sponsored/articles/aroundmytable. Accessed 15 Jan. 2022.

"Jocelyn and Meiko: Around My Table, Presented by Classico." *Food Network*, https://www.foodnetwork.com/sponsored/articles/aroundmytable. Accessed 15 Jan. 2022.

Johnson, Louise C. "Browsing the Modern Kitchen: A Feast of Gender, Place, and Culture." *Gender, Place and Culture*, vol. 13, no. 2, Apr. 2006, pp. 123–32. *ProQuest*, https:/doi.org/10.1080/09663690600573601.

Johnson, Stefanie K., and Juan M. Madera. "Sexual Harassment Is Pervasive in the Restaurant Industry. Here's What Needs to Change." *Harvard Business Review*, 18 Jan. 2018, https://hbr.org/2018/01/sexual-harassment-is-pervasive-in-the-restaurant-industry-heres-what-needs-to-change.

Johnston, Josée, and Shyon Baumann. *Foodies: Democracy and Distinction in the Gourmet Foodscape*. Routledge, 2010.

Jones, Sam. "Pamela Anderson Poster for PETA Urges Vegetarianism, Provocative Style." *The Guardian*, 22 Oct. 2010, https://www.theguardian.com/uk/2010/oct/22/pamela-anderson-poster-peta-vegetarianism.

Jones, Sarah. "The Food Blog That Sparked Delancey Celebrates 10 Years." *Seattle Magazine*, 27 Nov. 2019, https://www.seattlemag.com/article/food-blog-sparked-delancey-celebrates-10-years.

Jovanovski, Natalie. *Digesting Femininities: The Feminist Politics of Contemporary Food Culture*. Palgrave Macmillan, 2017.

Juhasz, Suzanne. "Towards a Theory of Form in Feminist Autobiography." *Women's Autobiography: Essays in Criticism*, edited by Estelle C. Jelinek. Indiana University Press, 1980, pp. 221–37.

The Julia Child Foundation for Gastronomy and Culinary Arts. https://juliachildfoundation.org/tv/. Accessed 15 Dec. 2020.

"Julia Child's Kitchen." *Smithsonian's National Museum of American History*, https://americanhistory.si.edu/food/julia-childs-kitchen. Accessed 15 Dec. 2020.

Bibliography

Kai Ellis, Jackie. *The Measure of My Powers: A Memoir of Food, Misery, and Paris.* Random House, 2018.

Karlsson, Lena. "Desperately Seeking Sameness: The Processes and Pleasures of Identification in Women's Diary Blog Reading." *Feminist Media Studies*, vol. 7, no. 2, 2007, pp. 137–53. *Taylor & Francis Online*, https:/doi.org/10.1080/14680770701287019.

Kelly, Traci Marie. "'If I Were a Voodoo Priestess': Women's Culinary Autobiographies." *Kitchen Culture in America: Popular Representations of Food, Gender, and Race*, edited by Sherrie Inness, University of Pennsylvania Press, 2001, pp. 251–69.

"Kerry Diamond." *Cherry Bombe*, https://cherrybombe.com/kerry-diamond. Accessed 21 Dec. 2020.

Kilbourne, Jean. *Can't Buy My Love: How Advertising Changes the Way We Think and Feel.* Simon & Schuster, 1999.

"*The Kitchen*—Jocelyn Delk Adams Makes Strawberry Cheesecake." *YouTube*, uploaded by grandbabycakes, 30 Jun. 2019, https://www.youtube.com/watch?app=desktop&v=D7pDyItX2Bg.

Klundt, Amanda. "*Gourmet* Magazine to Fold after 68 Years." *Eater*, 5 Oct. 2009, https://ny.eater.com/2009/10/5/6757851/gourmet-magazine-to-fold-after-68-years.

Kumar, Mousumi Saha. "Lisa Stone, Jory des Jardins and Elisa Camahort: The Founders of BlogHer, a Media Blog Network of Women." *Brainprick*, 16 Aug. 2012, http://brainprick.com/lisa-stone-jory-des-jardins-and-elisa-camahort-the-founders-of-blogher-a-media-blog-network-of-women/.

Lauter, David. "No Controversy Brews, Just Tea, as Mrs. Clinton Pours." *Los Angeles Times*, 17 Mar. 1993, https://www.latimes.com/archives/la-xpm-1993-03-17-mn-11962-story.html.

Lawson, Nigella. "Home Cooking Can Be a Feminist Act." *Lenny Letter*, 10 Apr. 2018, https://www.lennyletter.com/story/nigella-lawson-home-cooking-can-be-a-feminist-act.

Lawson, Nigella. *How to Be a Domestic Goddess.* Vintage, 2000.

Lawson, Nigella. *How to Eat: The Pleasures and Principals of Good Food.* Chatto & Windus, 1999.

Levin, Diane E., and Jean Kilbourne. *So Sexy So Soon: The New Sexualized Childhood and What Parents Can Do to Protect Their Kids.* Ballantine, 2008.

Lewis, Edna. *The Taste of Country Cooking.* 1976, Knopf, 2008.

Lokko, Lesley. *White Papers, Black Marks: Architecture, Race, and Culture.* Athlone, 2000.

Long, Lucy M., editor. *The Food and Folklore Reader.* Bloomsbury, 2015.

Mallgrave, Henry Francis, and David Goodman. *An Introduction to Architectural Theory: 1968–Present.* Wiley-Blackwell, 2011.

"Making Hillary an Issue." *Frontline*, 26 Mar. 1992, https://www.pbs.org/wgbh/pages/frontline/shows/clinton/etc/03261992.html.

Manring, M. M. *Slave in a Box: The Strange Career of Aunt Jemima*. University Press of Virginia, 1998.

Massey, Doreen. *Space, Place, and Gender*. University of Minnesota Press, 1994.

Matchar, Emily. *Homeward Bound: Why Women Are Embracing the New Domesticity*. Simon and Schuster, 2013.

Matchar, Emily. "The New Domesticity: Fun, Empowering, or a Step Back for American Women?" *Washington Post*, 25 Nov. 2011, https://www.washingtonpost.com/opinions/the-new-domesticity-fun-empowering-or-a-step-back-for-american-women/2011/11/18/gIQAqkg1vN_story.html.

Maynard, Micheline. "The Restaurant Industry Is Roiling as Sexual Harassment Scandals Claim More Chefs." *Forbes*, 14 Dec. 2017, https://www.forbes.com/sites/michelinemaynard/2017/12/14/the-restaurant-industry-is-roiling-as-the-sexual-harassment-scandal-claims-more-chefs/#5f1f373d5889. Accessed 4 Jan. 2021.

McAdams, Annalise. "*Any Other Mouth*: Writing the Hybrid Memoir." *Semantics Scholar*, https://www.semanticscholar.org/paper/Any-Other-Mouth%3A-Writing-the-Hybrid-Memoir-MacAdams/ee1eea5193f24523369b676222fad5a3c4f7c393. Accessed 21 Jan. 27.

McGee, Diane. *Writing the Meal: Dinner in the Fiction of Early Twentieth-Century Women Writers*. University of Toronto Press, 2001.

McHugh, Kathleen. *American Domesticity: From How-To Manual to Hollywood Melodrama*. Oxford University Press, 1999.

McKeever, Amy. "Jose Andres Launches Pepe, His First DC Food Truck." *Eater: Washington, DC*, 5 Mar. 2012, https://dc.eater.com/2012/3/5/6608287/jose-andres-launches-pepe-his-first-dc-food-truck.

Melucci, Giulia. *I Loved, I Lost, I Made Spaghetti: A Memoir of Good Food and Bad Boyfriends*. Grand Central, 2009.

Mendelsohn, Daniel. "But Enough about Me." Review of *Memoir: A History* for the *New Yorker*, by Ben Yagoda. *New Yorker*, 18 Jan. 2010, https://www.newyorker.com/magazine/2010/01/25/but-enough-about-me-2.

Mennell, Stephen, Anne Murcott, and Anneke van Otterloo. *The Sociology of Food: Eating, Diet, and Culture*. Sage Press, 1992.

Miller, Carolyn, R., and Dawn Shepherd. "Questions for Genre Theory from the Blogosphere." *Genres in the Internet: Issues in the Theory of Genre*, edited by Janet Giltrow and Dieter Stein, John Benjamins, 2009, pp. 88–115.

Miller, Jeff, and Jonathan Deutsch. *Food Studies: An Introduction to Research Methods*. Berg, 2009.

Mk. Comment on "*Cleaving: A Story of Marriage, Meat, and Obsession*." *Amazon*, 8 Dec. 2010, https://www.amazon.com/Cleaving-Story-Marriage-Meat-Obsession/dp/B005IV17EO.

Moses, Kate. *Cakewalk*. Dial, 2013.

Bibliography

Muhlke, Christine. "Kiss the Cook." *New York Times*, 3 Dec. 2009, https://www.nytimes.com/2009/12/06/books/review/Muhlke-t.html.

Mulvey, Laura. *Visual and Other Pleasures*. Palgrave McMillan, 2004.

"The National Organization for Women's 1966 Statement of Purpose." *National Organization for Women*, http://now.org/about/history/statement-of-purpose. Accessed 11 Jul. 2017.

Nettles-Barcelón, Kimberly D. "Women and Entrepreneurial Food-Work: Second Acts, 'New Domesticity,' and the Continuing Significance of Racialized Difference." *Food and Foodways*, vol. 25, no. 4, Nov. 2017, pp. 251–62. *Taylor & Francis Online*, https:/doi.org/10.1080/07409710.2017.1391023.

"*The New York Times* 14 Best Cookbooks of Fall 2020." *New York Times*, 29 Sep. 2020, https://www.nytimes.com/2020/09/29/dining/best-cookbooks.html.

Nigella Bites: Season One. Flashback Television, 2000.

"Nigella Lawson." *Wikipedia*, https://en.wikipedia.org/wiki/Nigella_Lawson. Accessed 22 Dec. 2020.

"NKBA Study Examines Average Kitchen Size in U.S." *KBIS*, 10 Oct. 2016, https://www.kbbonline.com/news/trends-inspirations/nkba-study-examines-average-kitchen-size-u-s/.

Nolan, Tom. "Following a Trail of Crumbs to Self-Understanding." *American Booksellers Association*, 4 Dec. 2007, https://www.bookweb.org/news/following-trail-crumbs-self-understanding.

"Not Becoming My Mother: Ruth Reichl." *Foratv.com*, http://library.fora.tv/2009/05/10/Not_Becoming_My_Mother_Ruth_Reichl. Accessed 11 Jul. 2017.

The Okra Project. https://www.theokraproject.com/. Accessed 21 Dec. 2020.

Ost, Carina. "The Eight Sexiest Women on TV Cooking Shows." *SF Weekly*, 15 Apr. 2011, https://www.sfweekly.com/dining/the-eight-sexiest-women-on-tv-cooking-shows/.

"Overview: The Annual NYWICI Matrix Awards." *New York Women in Communications, Inc.*, http://nywici.org/matrix. Accessed 11 Jul. 2017.

Parry, Jovian. "Gender and Slaughter in Popular Gastronomy." *Feminism & Psychology*, vol. 20, no. 3, 2010, pp. 381–97, https:/doi.org/10.1177/09593535 10368129.

Perelman, Deb. "best cocoa brownies." *Smitten Kitchen*, 20 Jan. 2010, https://smittenkitchen.com/2010/01/best-cocoa-brownies/.

Perelman, Deb. "freedom, ringing." *Smitten Kitchen*, 30 Jun. 2006, https://smittenkitchen.com/2006/06/freedom-ringing/.

Peretti, Jacques. "Too Hot to Handle." *The Guardian*, 29 Aug. 2000, https://www.theguardian.com/media/2000/aug/30/tvandradio.television4.

Peterson, William. "Success Story: Japanese American Style." *New York Times*, 9 Jan. 1966, https://www.nytimes.com/1966/01/09/archives/success-story-japaneseamerican-style-success-story-japaneseamerican.html.

Bibliography

Plante, Ellen M. *The American Kitchen, 1700 to the Present: From Hearth to Highrise*. Facts on File, 1995.

Pols, Mary. "Fret, Mull, Marry." *Time*, 18 Jan. 2010, pp. 63–65. *Academic Search Complete*, https://advance-lexis-com.proxygw.wrlc.org/api/document?collection=news&id=urn:contentItem:3SJ4-GBB0-000Y-N4M4-00000-00&context=1516831. Accessed 19 Oct. 2019.

Powell, Julie. *Cleaving: A Story of Marriage, Meat, and Obsession*. Little, Brown, 2009.

Powell, Julie. *Julie & Julia: 365 Days, 524 Recipes, 1 Tiny Apartment Kitchen*. Little, Brown, 2005.

Powell, Julie. *The Julie/Julia Project*, https://web.archive.org/web/20021217011704/http://blogs.salon.com/0001399/2002/08/25.html. Accessed 27 Jan. 2021.

Presswood, Alane L. "Constitutive Rhetoric and Digital Communities." *Food Blogs, Postfeminism, and the Communication of Expertise: Digital Domestics*, by Presswood. Lexington, 2020, pp 87–112.

Presswood, Alane L. *Food Blogs, Postfeminism, and the Communication of Expertise: Digital Domestics*. Lexington, 2020.

"Q&A With Jocelyn Delk Adams of Grandbaby Cakes." *Room&Board*, https://www.roomandboard.com/blog/2015/09/qa-jocelyn-delk-adams-grandbaby-cakes/. Accessed 20 Jan. 2022.

"Rachael Ray Bio." *Food Network*, https://www.foodnetwork.com/profiles/talent/rachael-ray/bio. Accessed 15 Dec. 2020.

Ramos, Alejandra. "*Julie & Julia*: An Edible Review" *Always Order Dessert*, 5 Aug. 2020, http://www.alwaysorderdessert.com/2009/08/julie-julia-edible-movie-review.html.

Rehak, Melanie. "The Power of Chow." *Bookforum*, https://www.bookforum.com/print/2203/ruth-reichl-endures-a-difficult-year-by-cooking-and-tweeting-14949. Accessed 5 Feb. 2021.

Reichl, Ruth, editor. *The Best American Food Writing*. 2018, Houghton Mifflin Harcourt, 2018.

Reichl, Ruth. *Comfort Me with Apples: More Adventures at the Table*. Random House, 2001.

Reichl, Ruth. *Delicious! A Novel*. Random House, 2014.

Reichl, Ruth. "A Departure for Alice's Restaurant." *Los Angeles Times*, 8 Feb. 1987, https://www.latimes.com/archives/la-xpm-1987-02-08-ca-1062-story.html.

Reichl, Ruth. *Garlic and Sapphires: The Secret Life of a Critic in Disguise*. Penguin Books, 2005.

Reichl, Ruth. "Gooey and Chewy." *Ruth Reichl*, 2 Jun. 2018, http://ruthreichl.com/about/.

Reichl, Ruth. *Mmmmm:. A Feastiary*. Rinehart and Winston, 1972.

Reichl, Ruth. *My Kitchen Year: 136 Recipes That Saved My Life*. Random House, 2015.

Reichl, Ruth. *Not Becoming My Mother: And Other Things She Taught Me along the Way*. Penguin Press, 2009.

Reichl, Ruth. *Save Me the Plums: My Gourmet Memoir*. Random House, 2019.

Reichl, Ruth. *Tender at the Bone: Growing Up at the Table*. Broadway Books, 1998.

Restaurant Opportunities Centers United. "Ending Jim Crow in America's Restaurants: Racial and Gender Occupational Segregation in the Restaurant Industry." *Restaurant Opportunities Centers United*. Oct. 2015, https://chapters.rocunited.org/wp-content/uploads/2015/10/RaceGender_Report_LR.pdfhttp://rocunited.org/publications/tipped-over-the-edge-gender-inequity-in-the-restaurant-industry.

Restaurant Opportunities Centers United. "Tipped over the Edge: Gender Inequity in the Restaurant Industry." *Restaurant Opportunities Centers United*, 13 Feb. 2012, http://rocunited.org/publications/tipped-over-the-edge-gender-inequity-in-the-restaurant-industry.

Rettberg, Jill Walker. *Blogging*. Polity, 2014.

Reuss, Carol. *Better Homes and Gardens and Its Editors: An Historical Study from the Magazine's Founding to 1970*. 1971. University of Iowa, PhD Dissertation.

Rewards Network. "Balancing Act: Navigating the Restaurant Workplace for Women." *Rewards Network*, https://www.rewardsnetwork.com/blog/balancing-act-navigating-restaurant-workplace-women/. Accessed 16 Sep. 2019.

Ro, Christine. "The Docility Myth Flattening Asian Women's Careers." *BBC Online*, 16 Aug. 2020, https://www.bbc.com/worklife/article/20200807-the-docility-myth-flattening-asian-womens-careers.

Robinson, Lynne. "50 of the World's Best Food Blogs." *London Times*, 17 Feb. 2019, https://www.thetimes.co.uk/article/50-of-the-worlds-best-food-blogs-fhq3plz6c55.

Robinson, Tasha. "Julie Powell: *Cleaving*." *A. V. Club*, 21 Jan. 2010, https://aux.avclub.com/julie-powell-cleaving-1798164145.

Rocheleau, Matt. "Chart: The Percentage of Women and Men in Each Profession." *Boston Globe*, 6 Mar. 2017, https://www2.bostonglobe.com/metro/2017/03/06/chart-the-percentage-women-and-men-each-profession/GBX22YsWloXaeHghwXfE4H/story.html.

Rodell, Besha. "Nigella Lawson Was Never Just a Domestic Goddess." *New York Times*, 19 Feb. 2019, https://www.nytimes.com/2019/02/19/dining/nigella-lawson.html.

Rodney, Alexandra, Sarah Cappeliez, Merin Oleschuk, and Josée Johnston. "The Online Domestic Goddess: An Analysis of Food Blog Femininities." *Food, Culture and Society*, vol. 20, no. 4, 2017, pp. 685–707. *Taylor & Francis Online*, doi.org/10.1080/15528014.2017.1357954.

Rothgerber, Hank. "Real Men Don't Eat (Vegetable) Quiche: Masculinity and the Justification of Meat Consumption." *Psychology of Men and Masculinity*, vol. 14, no. 4, 2013, pp. 363–76, https://doi.org/10.1037/a0030379.

"Ruth Reichl: About." *Ruth Reichl*, http://ruthreichl.com/about/. Accessed 18 Dec. 2020.

Ryans, Patrick. "Female Times: Food as Sex." *The Belfast News Letter*, 6 Sep. 2000, p. 26. *ProQuest*, http://proxygw.wrlc.org/login?url=https://www.proquest.com/newspapers/female-times-food-as-sex-one-ear-ground/docview/324629960/se-2.

"*Saveur's* 1st Annual Food Blog Awards: The Winners." *Saveur*, 5 Apr. 2010, https://www.saveur.com/article/Kitchen/SAVEURs-1st-Annual-Food-Blog-Awards-The-Winners/.

Sceats, Sarah. *Food, Consumption and the Body in Contemporary Women's Fiction.* Cambridge University Press, 2000.

Schneider, Michael. "Year in Review: Most-Watched Television Networks—Ranking 2020's Winners and Losers." *Variety*, 28 Dec. 2020, https://variety.com/2020/tv/news/network-ratings-2020-top-channels-fox-news-cnn-msnbc-cbs-1234866801/.

Schwartz Cowan, Ruth. *More Work for Mother: The Ironies of Household Technology from the Open Hearth to the Microwave.* Basic Books, 1983.

Scott, A. O. "Two for the Stove." *New York Times*, 6 Aug. 2020, https://www.nytimes.com/2009/08/07/movies/07julie.html.

Semega, Jessica, Melissa Kollar, Emily A. Shrider, and John Creamer. "Income and Poverty in the United States, 2019." *US Census Bureau*, 15 Sep. 2020, https://www.census.gov/library/publications/2020/demo/p60-270.html

Serfaty, Viviane. *The Mirror and the Veil: An Overview of American Diaries and Online Blogs.* Rodopi, 2004.

Severson, Kim. *Spoon Fed: How Eight Cooks Saved My Life.* Riverhead, 2010.

Severson, Kim and Julie Moskin. "Julie Powell, Food Writer Known for *Julie & Julia*, Dies at 49." *New York Times*, 1 Nov. 2022, https://www.nytimes.com/2022/11/01/dining/julie-powell-dead.html#:~:text=She%20was%2049.,rising%20generation%20of%20disaffected%20contemporaries.

Shapiro, Laura. *Perfection Salad: Women and Cooking at the Turn of the Century.* Farrar, Straus & Giroux, 1986.

Shapiro, Laura. *Something from the Oven: Reinventing Dinner in 1950s America.* Penguin, 2005.

Sharp, Leslie N. *Women Shaping Shelter: Technology, Consumption, and the Twentieth Century House.* 2004. Georgia Institute of Technology, PhD Dissertation.

Sharpless, Rebecca. *Cooking in Other Women's Kitchens: Domestic Workers in the South, 1865–1960.* University of North Carolina, 2010.

"Shauna Ahern: Founder and CEO, glutenfreegirl.com." General Assembly, https://generalassemb.ly/instructors/shauna-ahern/5755#:~:text=Gluten%2DFree%20Girl%20and%20the,her%20website%20to%20book%20form. Accessed 14 Nov. 2022.

Bibliography

"Shelves>Food Writing>Popular Food Writing Books." *Goodreads*, 20 Dec. 2021, https://www.goodreads.com/shelf/show/food-writing.

Smith, Caroline. *Cosmopolitan Culture and Consumerism in Chick Lit*. Routledge, 2008.

Smith, Sidonie. *A Poetics of Women's Autobiography: Marginality and the Fictions of Self-Representation*. Indiana University Press, 1987.

Sobal, Jeffery. "Men, Meat, and Marriage: Models of Masculinity." *Food and Foodways*, vol. 13, no. 1–2, 2005, pp. 135–38. *MLA International Bibliography*, https:/doi.org/10.1080/07409710590915409.

Spain, Daphne. *Gendered Spaces*. University of North Carolina Press, 1992.

Spence, Shay. "These Are the Sexiest Male Chefs in America 2017." *People*, 16 Nov. 2017, https://people.com/food/sexiest-chefs-america-2017/.

Sterling, Colin. "Ruth Reichl Memoir Title Changed from 'Not Becoming My Mother' to 'For You, Mom. Finally.'" *Huffington Post*, 3 Mar. 2011, http://www.huffingtonpost.com/2010/04/21/ruth-reichl-memoir-title_n_546128.html.

Strasser, Susan. *Never Done: A History of American Housework*. Pantheon Books, 1982.

Sunée, Kim. *Trail of Crumbs: Hunger, Love, and the Search for Home*. Grand Central, 2008.

"Target Launches Giada De Laurentiis for Target." *Target Addict*, 10 Jan. 2010, http://target-addict.blogspot.com/2010/01/target-launches-giada-de-laurentiis-for.html.

Tax, Meredith. "Songs," http://www.meredithtax.org/songs. Accessed 11 Jul. 2017.

Tax, Meredith. "There was a young woman who swallowed a lie. . . ." *Duke University Special Collections Library. Women's Liberation Movement*, http://library.duke.edu/digitalcollections/wlmpc_wlmmso1010/. Accessed 11 Jul. 2017.

Temple, Meiko. Meiko and the Dish, https://meikoandthedish.com/. Accessed 29 Aug. 2022.

Theophano, Janet. *Eat My Words: Reading Women's Lives Through the Cookbooks They Wrote*. Palgrave, 2002.

Torre, Susana. *Women in American Architecture*. Whitney Library of Design, 1977.

Turshen, Julia. *Feed the Resistance: Recipes and Ideas for Getting Involved*. Chronicle Books, 2017.

Turshen, Julia. "To Change Racial Disparity in Food, Let's Start with Cookbooks." *Eater*, 5 Apr. 2018, https://www.eater.com/2018/4/5/17153806/racial-inequality-food-cookbook-authors-publishing.

"The Twelfth Annual Weblog Awards: The 2012 Bloggies." *The Weblog Awards*, http://2012.bloggi.es/. Accessed 23 Jan. 2021.

"The 20 Best Food Books from 2001–2017." *The Guardian*, 21 Jan. 2018, https://www.theguardian.com/lifeandstyle/2018/jan/21/20-best-food-books-2001-to-2017.

"2014 Book Awards Recap." *The James Beard Foundation*, 2 May 2014, https://www.jamesbeard.org/blog/2014-book-awards-recap.

Van der Merwe, Chris N., and Hein Viljoen. *Beyond the Threshold: Explorations of Liminality in Literature*. Peter Lang, 2007.

Van Slooten, Jessica Lyn. "A Marriage Made in the Kitchen: Amanda Hesser's *Cooking for Mr. Latte* and Julie Powell's *Julie & Julia* as Foodie Romance." *You Are What You Eat: Literary Probes into the Palate*, edited by Annette M. Magid, Cambridge Scholars, 2008, pp. 367–408.

Waldrep, Shelton. *In the Dissolution of Place: Architecture, Identity, and Body*. Ashgate, 2013.

Walker, Lynne. "Home Making: An Architectural Perspective." *Signs*, vol. 13, no. 2, spring 2002, pp. 823–35. *JSTOR*, https://doi.org/10.1086/337927.

Walker, Rebecca. "Becoming the Third Wave." *Ms. Magazine*, Jan./Feb. 1992, pp. 39–41.

Wang, Qi. *The Autobiographical Self in Time and Culture*. Oxford, 2013.

Watt, Jenn. "Blogging Busts Out for Women." *Herizons*, 1 Jun. 2006, p. 7. *Academic Search Complete*, http://web.a.ebscohost.com.proxygw.wrlc.org/ehost/pdf viewer/pdfviewer?vid=3&sid=fb9fef38-8e00-46f1-b5fc-24a69d315d50%40s dc-v-sessmgr03. Accessed 22 Jan. 2021.

"Who Is Erin McKenna?" Erin McKenna's Bakery, http://www.erinmckennas bakery.com/story. Accessed 18 Mar. 2020.

Wida, Erica Chayes. "How baker Jocelyn Delk Adams found success by staying true to her matriarchal roots." *Today*, 9 Apr. 2001, https://www.today.com /tmrw/how-baker-joceyln-delk-adams-found-success-staying-true-her -t214377.

Wilson, Bee. "Kitchen Revolution: How Nigella Lawson Changed Food Writing." *The Guardian*, 6 Oct. 2018, https://www.theguardian.com/books/2018/oct/06 /how-nigella-lawson-changed-food-writing.

Wizenberg, Molly. *Delancey: A Man, A Woman, A Restaurant, A Marriage*. Simon & Schuster, 2014.

Wizenberg, Molly. *The Fixed Stars*. Abrams, 2020.

Wizenberg, Molly. *A Homemade Life: Stories and Recipes from My Kitchen Table*. Simon & Schuster, 2013.

Wizenberg, Molly. *Orangette*, http://orangette.net/. Accessed 22 Dec. 2020.

Wu, Elaine. "RE: BlogHer Conference Statistics." Received by Caroline Smith, 10 Aug. 2012.

Yabroff, Jennie. "Touchy-Feely Food Memoirs." *Newsweek*, 8 Apr. 2010, https://www.newsweek.com/touchy-feely-food-memoirs-70495.

Zak, Dan. "'This Is My Baby': Michelle Obama's Last Spring Planting at the White House Garden." *Washington Post*, 5 Apr. 2019, https://www.washingtonpost .com/lifestyle/style/this-is-my-baby-michelle-obamas-last-spring-planting -at-the-white-house-garden/2016/04/05/51c8aff8-fb46-11e5-80e4-c381214de1a3 _story.html.

INDEX

ABC News, 50
absent referent, women as, 92–93
Abu-Jaber, Diana, 63
Acton, Eliza, 128n12
Adams, Amy, 3, 89, 103
Adams, Carol J., 92–94, 99, 103–4
Afroculinaria, 110
Ahern, Daniel, 111, 130n26
Ahern, Shauna James, 8, 17–18, 52–53, 57, 59, 64, 73–74, 107, 110, 113–14, 116, 118–20, 130n26; awards won, 111; celiac disease, 74, 107, 112
Alchemy of Genres, An (Freedman), 117
Allison, Dorothy, 10
Always Order Dessert (Ramos), 3
Amazon, 89–90
American Cookery (Simmons), 128n12
American Domesticity (McHugh), 102
American Kitchen, 1700 to the Present, The (Plante), 25
Anderson, Pamela, 99, 103
Anderson, Sunny, 66
Andino, Jordan, 134–35n5
Andrés, José, 128n11
Andrews, Colman, 43, 46–47
Angelou, Maya, 10
Animal, Vegetable, Miracle (Kingsolver), 7

"Any Other Mouth: Writing the Hybrid Memoir" (McAdams), 116–17
Around My Table, 62
Art of Eating In, The (Erway), 73
Atkinson, Piers, 65
A.V. Club, 90
Avakian, Arlene, 10–11

Babycakes, 52–53, 113
Bacon Show, The, 110
Bakers against Racism, 65–66
Barclay, Eliza, 105–6
Bard, Elizabeth, 17, 103
Barthes, Roland, 10
Batali, Mario, 101
Bauermeister, Erica, 6
Baumann, Shyon, 63
Baussan, Olivier, 79–86, 135n14
BBC, 135n15
Beautiful, Terrible Thing, A (Waite), 73
Beeton, Isabella, 128n12
Belasco, Warren, 9, 18
Belfast News Letters, 69
Bennett, Natalie, 107–8
Berkely Arts and Letters program, 132n3
Best American Food Writing, The (Reichl), 5, 127n3

155

156 Index

Best Recipes in the World, The (Bittman), 7

Better Homes and Gardens, 13, 21–36, 62; advertisements, 1960s, 28; advertisements, 1970s, 29; advertisements, 2000s, 32; April 1970, 30; April 1980, 30–31; April 2010, 34; August 1960, 29; August 1970, 30; blueprints, 22–23, 35, 130n1; cultural messaging, 27–28; February 1960, 29, 33; February 1980, 30; February 1990, 33–34; "Idea Home of the Year," 35–36; January 1970, 29–30; January 1990, 31; January 2000, 31, 34; January 2010, 31–32; kitchens in, 14, 21–23, 26–36, 113, 132n15; launching of, 27; March 1960, 33; March 2010, 34; May 1960, 21–22, 28, 33; May 1970, 30; May 1990, 34; media kit, 27; November 1970, 30; readership, 13–14, 27, 33, 34, 129n22, 131n11, 132n19; September 1957, 35–36; September 1990, 31; September 2000, 31–32; September 2010, 32, 34–35; website, 22, 130n1

Better Homes and Gardens and Its Editors (Reuss), 27

Betty Crocker Show, 40–41

Betty Crocker's Cookbook, 128n12

Big Bowl Cookbook (Cost), 125

Bitch, 15, 51, 53–55; kitschy advertisements in, 54

Bittman, Mark, 7, 128n13

Black Lives Matter, 63, 66

Blogger (self-publishing service), 107

"Bloggers Replace Mom's Recipe Box as Source of Food Knowledge" (Barclay), 105, 106

"Blogging Busts Out for Women" (Watt), 107; women and, 107–8

BlogHer, 108; conference, 109; Food Network, 109; Network, 108–9

blogs, 105–20, 128n14; audience, 116; community, 119–20; definition of, 114; feminist, 107–8; food, 3, 4, 7–9, 15, 17–18, 51, 57, 64, 65, 72, 109–20; formal elements of, 118; publication order, 116

Blood, Bones, Butter (Hamilton), 8

Bloom, Lynn Z., 6, 11

body policing, 69–71

Bollen, Christopher, 53

Bon Appétit, 62, 63

Bookforum, 124

Bookslut.com, 73

Bordo, Susan, 10, 70

Boston Cooking School Handbook, The (Farmer), 128n12

Boston Globe, 102

Bourdain, Anthony, 7, 124

Bradley, Patricia, 55

Bravo, 5–6

Bread and Roses, 133n4

Bridget Jones's Diary (Fielding), 72

Brinson, Rob, 34–35

Brown, Jerry, 49

"Browsing the Modern Kitchen" (Johnson), 25

Buch, Clarissa, 100–101

Buchtenkirch-Biscardi, Lyde, 136n3

Bullock-Prado, Gesine, 64, 73

Bureau of Statistics, 100

Bush, Barbara, 50

Bushnell, Candace, 72

BUST, 15, 51, 53–56; Spring 2004, 54

Byrne, David, 115

Cairns, Kate, 129n18

Cakewalk (Moses), 7–8, 73

Camahort, Elisa, 108

Can't Buy My Love (Kilbourne), 70

CapMac, 128n11

Carman, Tim, 128n10

Carnival of Feminists, 107

Index

Carter, Ethan, 106
celebrity food culture, 5, 6, 63, 65–69, 71, 101; obsession with weight in, 69; racism in, 63–64; sexism in, 63–64, 69
Cesiri, Daniela, 118
Charles, Robert, 48
Cherry Bombe magazine, 65–66, 134nn7–8; Cherry Bombe University, 134n8; Jubilee, 134n8
Chiang, Cecilia, 63
chick lit, 16, 55, 72, 74, 103
Chicken-n-Beer (Ludacris album), 103
Child, Julia, 3–4, 7, 72, 89, 113, 128n12
Chopin, Kate, 11
Classico, 62
Cleaving (Powell), 17, 89–104; affair with D, 91, 94–95, 97; association between women and animals in, 91–92, 94, 96, 97; connections between sex and butchery in, 91–92, 95–97; gender politics in, 90–91, 95–97, 99, 103–4; illustrations in, 98–99; recipes in, 98; reviews of, 89–90, 95–96; sexual assault in, 97–98
Clicks & Cravings, 105
Clifford, Stephanie, 121
Climbing the Mango Trees (Jaffrey), 8
Clinton, Bill, 49
Clinton, Hillary, 49–50
Coach, 133n7
Colicchio, Tom, 7, 128n13
Colomina, Beatriz, 23–24
Colwin, Laurie, 9
Comfort Me with Apples (Reichl), 7, 14, 37, 39–40, 123; cooking as an act of rebellion in, 43–44; gender/class politics in, 41–45; "The Other Side of the Bridge," 41–42; recipes in, 47–48
computer-mediated communication (CMC), 118

Conant, Scott, 127n5
Condé Nast, 121
Cone, Diana, 98
"Consuming Prose" (Bloom), 6
cookbooks, 6, 7, 11, 16–18, 40, 48, 107, 110, 115–16, 118, 122, 125; print, 106; racial biases in, 64–65
Cooking Channel, 134–35n5
Cooking for Mr. Latte (Hesser), 17, 103
Cooking Lessons (Inness), 129n18
Coontz, Stephanie, 28
Cooper, Ann, 99–100, 136n3
Coppola, Sofia, 65
Cortina, Melissa, 102
Cost, Bruce, 44, 46, 125
Counihan, Carole, 9, 10
Couric, Katie, 109
Cromley, Elizabeth Collins, 25–26, 131n10
Culinary Institute of America, 136n3
Curbside Cupcakes, 128n11

Daily Telegraph, 68
DATA USA, 102
David Lebovitz, 110
Davis, Camas, 65
De Laurentiis, Giada, 69, 127–28n8, 134n5
Deck, Alice A., 60, 61
Deen, Paula, 63
Dekker, Cynthia and Jack, 34
Delancey (Wizenberg), 111
Delicious! (Reichl), 18, 39, 48, 122–24
Delk Adams, Jocelyn, 15–16, 51–52, 57–59, 62–63, 65, 113; activism, 66; recoding housewife persona, 15–16, 51–52, 58–62; television appearances, 59–63
Department of Urban and Environmental Planning, School of Architecture, University of Virginia, 24

Des Jardins, Jory, 108

Design Futuring (Fry), 52–53, 129n24, 133n1

"Desperately Seeking Sameness" (Karlsson), 114

Deutsch, Jonathan, 10

Diamond, Jason, 122

Diamond, John, 134n3

Diamond, Kerry, 65, 133–34n7

diaries, 5, 17, 107, 114–16

Dickinson, Emily, 11

Digesting Femininities (Jovanovski), 70–72, 74

Dinner Roles (Inness), 11

Discourse of Food Blogs, The (Cesiri), 118

domestic advice manuals, 26

Domestic Cultures (Hollows), 39

domestic science movement, 26

domesticity, new, 55–56, 133n4

Domitrovich, Michael, 7

Doomsday Vault, 65

Dr. Oz, 62

Drummond, Ree, 64

Duff, David, 116

Duke University, 132–33n4

Dunham, Lena, 87

Dunlop, Fuchsia, 8

Dutton, Rachel, 65

E!, 67

Eagleton, Mary, 117

Eastman, Max, 132n2

Eat, Pray, Love (Gilbert), 128n9

Eat Pray Love (movie), 128n9

Eater, 64, 121

Ebony magazine, 62

"Eight Sexiest Women on Cooking Shows, The," 69, 134n5

Ellis, Jackie Kai, 73

Enough (Ahern), 111

Ephron, Nora, 3

Erway, Cathy, 73

F Word, The, 95

Facebook, 129n17

Fain, Lisa, 128n14

Family Circle, 50

Farmer, Fannie, 128n12

fashion industry, 70

Fearing, Dean, 127n5

Feed the Resistance (Turshen), 64

"Feeling Like a Domestic Goddess" (Hollows), 68, 135n8

Felton, Lena, 63

Feminine Mystique, The (Friedan), 38, 41, 56, 59–60; "A New Life Plan for Women," 41

Feminism, Domesticity, and Popular Culture (Gillis & Hollows), 38–39

feminism and feminist scholarship, 10–11, 37–48, 71; aims of, 38–39; architecture and, 24, 25; blogs, 107–8; domesticity and, 38–39; literary scholarship, 117–18; second wave, 13–15, 27, 38–39, 44–46, 51, 57; third wave, 15, 51, 53–55, 57, 129n23; women's appetites and, 70–71

Feminism & Psychology, 95–96

Fey, Tina, 54

Fielding, Helen, 72

Fields, Kelly, 133n6

first ladies, changing roles of, 49–50

Fisher, M. K., 9

Fixed Stars, The (Wizenberg), 111

Flagg, Fannie, 11

Flay, Bobby, 127n8

Fleisher's (butcher shop), 91, 94, 97, 103

Flinders, Carol, 119–20

Flinn, Kathleen, 8, 73

Food, Inc. (Kenner), 6

Food and Culture (Counihan & Van Esterik), 9–10

Food and Femininity (Cairns & Johnston), 129n18

Index 159

Food and Folklore Reader, The (Long), 9–10
Food and Foodways, 96
food axis, 25
Food Axis, The (Cromley), 25, 26
Food Blogs, Post-Feminism, and the Communication of Expertise (Presswood), 8, 110
Food Network, 5, 59, 62–63, 127n6, 128n8
Food Studies: An Introduction to Research Methods (Miller & Deutsch), 10
Food: The Key Concepts (Belasco), 9, 18
food trucks, 6, 128n11
foodie romances, 17, 89–104
Foodies (Johnston & Baumann), 63
For You Mom, Finally (Reichl), 132n1
Fortune Cookie Chronicles (Lee), 7
Fortune magazine, 108
Foxwoods Casino, 131n6
Frank, Anne, 116
Freedman, Diane P., 117
French Chef, The, 4
Fried Green Tomatoes at the Whistle Stop Café (Flagg), 11
Friedan, Betty, 13, 38, 41–45, 46, 51, 53, 59–60
Friedman, Ken, 101
From Betty Crocker to Feminist Food Studies (Avakian & Haber), 11
Fruit, Garden, and Home, 27
Fry, Tony, 52–53, 129n24, 133n1

gardening, 6, 128n10
Garfinkel, Nancy, 6
Garlic and Sapphires (Reichl), 7, 37, 123, 138n1; "Molly," 123
Garten, Ina, 66, 86–87, 133n6
Garten, Jeffrey, 87
Gee, Denise, 34–35
gender: and environments/spaces, 24–25, 50–51; inequalities, 39; and

politics of the kitchen, 5, 24–26, 32–33, 35–36, 39, 50–51, 87, 99–100, 102
"Gender and Genre" (Eagleton), 117
"Gender and Slaughter in Popular Gastronomy" (Parry), 95–96
Gendered Spaces (Spain), 24
General Mills, 40
genre theory, 117
G.I. Joe, 3
Gigliotti, Lynne, 136n3
Gilbert, Elizabeth, 128n9
Gillis, Stacey, 38–39
Gluten-Free Girl, 8, 17, 52, 64, 73–74, 107, 110, 115; "Eating Vegan with Tomato-Fennel Soup," 119; first post, 112; reader comments on, 118–19; recipes, 115; "Souffle, Slowly, Sunday Afternoon, with Molly," 119; "Two Loves, Both a Little Silly, But I'm Besotted," 113
Gluten-Free Girl American Classics Revisited (Ahern), 111
Gluten-Free Girl and the Chef (Ahern), 111, 130n26
Gluten-Free Girl Every Day (Ahern), 111
Gluten-Free Girl: How I Found the Food That Loves Me Back and How You Can Too (Ahern), 111
Godfrey, Bronwen, 120
Goeller, Alison D., 11
Goin, Suzanne, 127n5
Gold, Jonathan, 125
Goldman-Moore, Mila, 35
Good Housekeeping, 60
Goodreads, 8
Goodwin, Julie, 71
Gordon, Megan, 105–6
Gourmet magazine, 5, 38, 48, 68, 124, 127n5; closing, 121, 122, 124
Gramercy Tavern, 128n13

Grandbaby Cakes (blog), 15, 51, 58–59, 62; merchandise, 59
Grandbaby Cakes (Delk Adams), 16, 51, 58–59; family histories in, 57–58, 62; recipes in, 58–59, 62
Granof, Victoria, 65
Gras, Laurent, 127n5
Great American Baking Show, The, 101
Groeneveld, Elizabeth, 53–57, 133n3
Grubhub, 100
Guardian, The, 64, 68–69, 133n6
Guignery, Vanessa, 117

Haber, Barbara, 11
Hall, Carla, 63, 66
Halloran, Vivian Nun, 11–12
Hamilton, Gabrielle, 8, 65, 129n16
Hanisch, Carol, 13
Hansen, Marjorie, 26
Happy Little Bento, 110
Harper's Bazaar, 133–34n7
Hartman Group, 105
Harvard Business Review, 101
Harvard University, 65
Hassan, Hawa, 65, 133n6
Hawbaker, K. T., 86–87, 136nn18–19
HBO, 103
Heart of Dinner, 66
Heller, Tamar, 70
Henry, Diana, 67–68
Hesser, Amanda, 12, 17, 103, 129n21
Hillside Club, 132n3
Hirschberg, Lynn, 68, 69
Hollis, Doug, 40, 42–44, 46, 47
Hollows, Joanne, 38–39, 135n8
Holmes, Linda, 90
Homemade Life, A (Wizenberg), 111
Homesick Texan, 128n14
Homeward Bound (Matchar), 55–56
"Hottest Women of the Food Network, The," 69
Houghton Mifflin Harcourt, 127n3

House and Garden, 27
House Beautiful, 27
housewives, 13–14, 18, 37–48; advertising and, 40–41, 59–61; expectations of, 50–51, 132n2; "happy housewife heroine," 15–16, 38, 40, 42–43, 46, 51, 53, 56, 59–60; post–World War II, 37–38, 40–41; race and, 15–16, 51–52, 58–62; recoding the image of, 56–62
Houzz, 22
"How Nigella Lawson and Ina Garten Helped Me Love My Fat, Queer Self" (Hawbaker), 86–87
How to Be a Domestic Goddess (Lawson), 68
How to Eat (Lawson), 68
hybrid genres, 12, 18, 114, 116–17
Hybridity: Forms and Figures in Literary and the Visual Arts (Guignery), 117

"I Got It from My Mama" (will.i.am (song), 59
I Loved, I Lost, I Made Spaghetti (Melucci), 16, 70, 74–79; body imagery in, 75–76; conflation of sex with food in, 74–75; ending of, 78–79; recipes in, 79, 135n13; role of feeder in, 75–78; "Single Girl Suppers," 78
I Shop Therefore I Am (Kruger), 53
identity and identity politics, 11–12; building design and, 24–25, 130–31n6, 131n9; ethnic, 16–17
Immigrant Kitchen, The (Halloran), 11–12
In Defense of Food (Pollan), 7
In Julia's Kitchen with Master Chefs, 4
"In Search of Our Mother's Gardens" (Walker), 10
Inge, Leoneda, 101
Inness, Sherrie, 11, 129n18

Index

Instagram, 129n17
Interview, 53
Iron Chef America, 5
Israel, Andrea, 6
Iuzzini, Johnny, 101

J. Lyons & Co., 134n3
Jaffrey, Madhur, 8, 12, 63, 134n8
James Beard Award: for Focus on
    Health, 111; for Individual Food
    Blog, 111
Jamie's Great Italian Escape, 95
Johnson, Louise C., 25, 131n9
Johnson, Philip, 131n6
Johnston, Josée, 63, 129n18
Jones, Judith, 9, 65
Jovanovski, Natalie, 70–72, 74–75,
    77–78, 135n8
Joy of Cooking, The, 128n12
Joy the Baker, 134
Juhaz, Suzanne, 114–15
Julie & Julia (movie), 3, 6, 89, 128n9
Julie & Julia (Powell), 3, 8, 17, 72, 89–92,
    102
Julie/Julia Project, The, 3–4, 17, 64, 89,
    129n21
Jurgensen, Dalia, 7

Karlsson, Lena, 114
Keenan, Jenny and Joe, 34
Kelly, Traci Marie, 11
Kenner, Robert, 6
Kerr, Robert, 24–25
Kilbourne, Jean, 70
Killingsworth, Silvia, 5
Kingsolver, Barbara, 7
Kish, Kristen, 65
kitchen: colonial, 25; as "command
    post," 26; cultural context of, 23;
    efficiency over style, 28–30; gen-
    der politics of, 5, 24–26, 32–33,
    35–36, 39, 50–51, 87, 99–100, 102;

instruction manuals, 128n12; intel-
    ligent, 32; marginalizing of, 26,
    29–30, 32; multipurpose, 25; open,
    26, 30–31, 132n16; physical design
    of, 23, 25–26, 30–31, 39; placement
    of, 23, 25–26; recoding of, 49–66;
    renovations, 22, 30; role in home,
    21–22, 30–31; role in women's lives,
    10, 13–14; space, 4, 12–13, 21–36,
    39, 113, 123–24, 131n10; as space for
    growth and development, 70–87;
    super, 22, 32; versus living space in
    home, 22–23, 26, 28–31, 35–36
Kitchen, The, 59, 62
Kitchen and Bath, 28–29
Kitchen Confidential (Bourdain), 7
Kitchen Culture in America (Inness),
    129n18
Kiwi Kitchen, 95
Kloss, Karlie, 65
Klundt, Amanda, 121
knitting, 55–56, 133n3
Kohl's, 127n8
Kondo, Marie, 63
Kruger, Barbara, 53
Kurlansky, Mark, 7
Kwolek-Folland, Angel, 24

Ladies Home Journal, 96
Lakshmi, Padma, 69
Lancôme, 133n7
Laurel's Kitchen (Robertson, Flinders,
    & Godfrey), 119–20
Lawson, Nigel, 134n3
Lawson, Nigella, 67–68, 71, 75, 86–87,
    134nn2–3; messaging about women
    and food, 68–69, 87, 135n8; sur-
    veillance of personal appearance,
    68–69, 71–72, 134n5
Lawson, Vanessa, 134n3
Le Cordon Bleu, 73
Lebovitz, David, 110

162 Index

Lee, Jennifer, 7
Lee, Lara, 133n6
Lenny Letter, 87
Let's Move! campaign, 6
Lewis, Edna, 128n12
Lily, The, 63
Literary Hub, 122
Little, Brown & Company, 3
L'Occitane en Provence, 135n14
Lokko, Lesley Naa Norle, 130–31n6
London Times, 111
Long, Lucy M., 9–10
Los Angeles Times, 5, 14, 38–39, 122, 125, 133n5
Ludacris, 103
Lunch in Paris (Bard), 17, 103

Machado, Eduardo, 7, 12
Madeloni, Marita, 106
Making Feminist Media (Groeneveld), 53–55
male gaze, 69, 71–72, 134n4, 136n19
manifestos, 7
Manring, M. M., 61
"Marriage Made in the Kitchen, A" (Van Slooten), 102–3
Mastering the Art of French Cooking (Child), 3–4, 72, 89
Matchar, Emily, 55–56
Matrix Award, 38, 132n3
Mauer, Lisa J., 65
McAdams, Annalise, 116–17
McCall's, 59–60
McCarty, Michael, 44, 46, 48
McHugh, Kathleen Anne, 102
McKenna, Erin, 52–53, 57, 60, 65, 113
Me magazine, 134n7
Mead, Margaret, 10
Measure of My Powers, The (Ellis), 73
meat industry, women in, 102
Media Decoder, 121

Media Report to Women, 108
Melucci, Guilia, 16, 70, 72, 74–79, 85, 87, 113
Memoir: A History (Yagoda), 107
memoir/autobiography, food, 5, 7–9, 11–12, 14, 18, 23, 27, 37, 39–40, 70–87, 103, 106, 110–11, 116, 122–23; hybrid, 116–17; marketing, 72–73; second act, 64, 124; as site of resistance, 72
"Men, Meat, and Marriage Models of Masculinity" (Sobal), 96
Mendelsohn, Daniel, 107
Men's Health, 97
Meredith, Edwin Thomas, 27
Merriam-Webster dictionary, 114
#MeToo movement, 101
Metropolitan Home, 44
Miller, Jeff, 10
Millet, Kate, 13
Mills, Alan, 133n4
Mintz, Sidney, 10
Mirror and the Veil, The (Serfaty), 115–16
Mmmmm: A Feastiary (Reichl), 39–40, 122
model minority, 135n15
Modern Cookery for Private Families (Acton), 128n12
Modern Genre Theory (Duff), 116
Moore, Waco, 35
Moran, Patricia, 70
More Adventures at the Table (Reichl), 7
Morley, Christopher, 132n2
Moses, Kate, 7–8, 73
Mr. Spots Chai House, 119
Mrs. Beeton's Book of Household Management (Beeton), 128n12
Muhlke, Christine, 90
Mulvey, Laura, 134n4
My Kitchen Year (Reichl), 18, 39, 48, 122, 124

My Life from Scratch (Bullock-Prado), 64, 73

National Gardening Association, 128n10
National Kitchen & Bath Association (NKBA), 29
National Organization of Women (NOW), 44–45
National Restaurant Association, 100
National Women's Law Center, 102
neo-crafting, 55–57
Nettles-Barcelón, Kimberly D., 11, 15, 64
New West magazine, 14, 39, 41, 43, 46, 122
New York Times, 3, 5, 38, 67, 90, 121, 122, 123, 128n13, 129n21, 135n15; "The 14 Best Cookbooks of Fall 2020," 64–65
New York Times Magazine, 68
New York Women in Communication, 132n3
New Yorker, 7
Newsweek, 8
Next Food Network Star, The, 5
Nigella Bites, 67–68, 134n2
"Nigella Lawson: Home Cooking Can Be a Feminist Art" (Hawbaker), 87
Nightline, 50
Nolan, Tom, 85
Nolon, Nikolai, 137n7
Nosra, Samin, 64
Not Becoming My Mother (Reichl), 37–38
"Now Then—Who Said Biscuits?" (Deck), 60
NPR, 90, 101, 105, 106

O Magazine, 62
Obama, Barack, 109
Obama, Michelle, 6, 128n10

O'Brien, Patricia, 50
Observer, The, 100
Okra Project, 66
101 Cookbooks, 129n17
oppositional structures/binaries, 4–5, 9, 12–13, 18, 26, 38–39, 41–42, 44–45, 47, 51, 93–94, 106, 114
Orangette, 17, 64, 72, 107, 110, 115; awards, 110–11; "Bigger and Fuller and Brighter," 119; "On Sharing a Sugar, with a Lot of Banana Cake," 112–13; reader comments, 119; recipes, 112, 115; "Sir Bones: Is Stuffed,/De World, Wif Feeding Girls," 119
organic food, 6
Orphan (design firm), 134n7

Paradez, Petra, 133n6
Parry, Jovian, 95–96
Pascale, Lorraine, 69
Paska, Megan, 56
Pearce and Pearce (building firm), 26
People magazine, 134–35n5
Pepe (food truck), 128n11
Perelman, Deb, 8, 64, 128n14
Peretti, Jacques, 69
PETA, 99, 103
Peterson, William, 135n15
Pew Research Center, 131n12
Piercy, Marge, 10
Pilaf, Pozole, and Pad Thai (Inness), 129n18
Pioneer Woman, The (Drummond), 64
Plante, Ellen M., 25–26, 131n10
Plath, Sylvia, 116
Playboar, 93
Playboy, 93
Pollan, Michael, 7, 129n15
Pols, Mary, 90
Polzine, Michelle, 133n6

164 Index

Pornography of Meat, The (Adams), 92, 103
Portland Meat Collective, 65
Powell, Eric, 3, 89–91, 97
Powell, Julie, 3, 8, 12, 17, 64, 72, 89–104, 113, 129n21, 137n7
Presswood, Alane L., 8, 110
Prune, 129n16
Psyche Therapy, 54
Publicis Consultants USA, 105
Puck, Wolfgang, 46, 48

Rachel Ray Show, 62
Radar Online, 69
Ramos, Alejandra, 3
Ramsay, Gordon, 69
Ramsey, Tara, 71
Ray, Rachel, 7, 66, 69, 121, 128n8
"Real Men Don't Eat (Vegetable) Quiche" (Rothgerber), 96–97
Recipe Club, The (Israel & Garfinkel), 6
recipe writing, 5, 12; print, 106
recoding, 133n1; definition, 53; kitchen space, 49–66; visual, 54, 56, 61–62
Red Hook Lobster, 128n11
Rehak, Melanie, 124
Reichl, Ruth, 7, 8, 14–15, 18, 37–48, 65, 113, 129n15, 133n5; brother, 40; Channing Way home, 41–44, 47; father, 42; at *Gourmet*, 38, 48, 121–26, 127n5; Matrix Award, 38, 132n3; mother, 37–38, 40–42, 123–24, 132n2; Twitter profile, 124–25; website, 40, 125
Repodepotfabrics.com, 54
restaurant industry: gender inequalities in, 99–102; sexual harassment in, 101
Restaurant Opportunities Centers United (ROC-United), 100, 136n4; "Ending Jim Crow in America's Restaurants," 100–101; "Tipped

Over the Edge—Gender Inequity in the Restaurant Industry," 100
Reuss, Carol, 27, 131n11
Rewards Network, 100
Ripert, Eric, 127n5
Ro, Christine, 135n15
Robertson, Laurel, 119–20
Robinson, Tasha, 90
Rodan, Claudia, 64
Rodell, Besha, 67
Roman, Alison, 63
Room and Board, 59
Rothgerber, Hank, 96–97
Routledge, 10
Ryans, Patrick, 69

Saffitz, Claire, 133n6
Sally Bingham Center for Women's History and Culture, 132–33n4
Salt, The, 101, 105
Salt: A World History of Food (Kurlansky), 7
Save Me the Plums (Reichl), 48, 121
Saveur, 7; 1st Annual Food Blog Awards (Bloggies), 110, 128n14, 137n7
Scenes of the Apple (Heller & Moran), 70
Schlosser, Eric, 10
School of Essential Ingredients, The (Bauermeister), 6
Scott, A. O., 3
Secret Ingredients (Inness), 11
"Seeds of Change" (Carman), 128n10
Serfaty, Viviane, 115–16
Severson, Kim, 8, 50, 51, 72
Sevigny, Chloe, 65
Sex and the City (Bushnell), 72
Sexual Politics of Meat, The (Adams), 92, 93
Sexuality and Space (Colomina), 23–24
Shapiro, Laura, 28, 40–41

Index 165

Shark's Fin and Sichuan Pepper (Dunlop), 8
Sharp, Leslie N., 24
Sharp Objects, 103–4, 137n7
Sharper Your Knife, the Less You Cry, The (Flinn), 8, 73
SHE Media, 108; Partner Network, 108
Sichuan Summit, 125
Simmons, Amelia, 128n12
Sitchinava, Nino, 22
Slave in a Box (Manring), 61
Smith Canteen, 134
Smitten Kitchen, 8, 64, 128n14
Sobal, Jeffery, 96
social media, 105–20, 129n17
Sodha, Meera, 64, 133n6
Something from the Oven (Shapiro), 28, 40–41
Spain, Daphne, 24–25
Spiced (Jurgensen), 7
Spoon Fed (Severson), 8, 50, 72
Steinem, Gloria, 13
Stewart, Martha, 7, 65–66, 113, 128n12
Stitch and Bitch (Stoller), 56
Stoller, Debbie, 56
Stone, Lisa, 108
Streep, Meryl, 3, 89
Style Network, 67
Sun, The, 69
Sunday Telegraph, 111
Sunée, Kim, 16, 70, 72, 79–87, 113; heritage, 80–82, 85–86, 129n25
superwoman syndrome, 26
Superwoman Syndrome (Hansen), 26
Swanson, Heidi J., 129n17
Sweeney, Dawn, 100

Tallman, Heather, 106
Target, 127n8
Tastes Like Cuba (Machado & Domitrovich), 7
Tax, Meredith, 45, 132–33n4

technological utopianism, 9
Temple, Meiko, 62
Tender at the Bone (Reichl), 7, 37, 40, 122–23
theKitchn, 105–6
"There Was a Young Woman Who Swallowed a Lie" (Tax), 45
"There Was an Old Woman Who Swallowed a Fly" (Mills), 133n4
Think Like a Chef (Colicchio), 7
Think Skateboards, 93
Through the Kitchen Window (Avakian), 10
Tiegen, Crissy, 63
Time magazine, 63, 90
Top Chef, 5, 69, 127n7, 128n13, 136n3; Top Chef University, 6
"Top 10 Female Chefs," 69
"Touchy-Feely Food Memoirs" (Yabroff), 8
"Towards a Theory of Form in Feminist Autobiography" (Juhaz), 114–15
Trail of Crumbs (Sunée), 16, 70, 79–86; feeling of displacement in, 79–80, 82, 84, 135–36n16; "Hungry After All," 86; kitchen space in, 81–82, 84–85; "The Monk's Table," 83–84; partner's expectations in, 80–83; power imbalance in, 81–84; race and identity in, 80–82, 85–86; recipes in, 81, 84–86; "A Room of One's Own," 85; "Where I Am," 82; "With Reservations," 84
True Detective, 103–4
Turlington Burns, Christy, 109
Turshen, Julia, 64, 66
Twitter, 122, 124–25
Twitty, Michael W., 110

Unbearable Weight (Bordo), 70
Underly, Kari, 101–2
UNICEF, 122–23

166 Index

University of Southern California, 50
Untitled (Connect) (Kruger), 53
US Census Bureau, 129n22
USDA, 128n10

V, 134n7
van der Merwe, Chris, 117
Van Esterik, Penny, 9, 10
Van Slooten, Jessica Lyn, 11–13, 17, 91, 102–3
Variety, 127n6
vegetarianism, 96–97
Velez, Paola, 65
Viljoen, Hein, 117
Visionaire, 134n7
"Visual Pleasure and Narrative Cinema" (Mulvey), 134n4
Vogue, 68, 121

Waite, Jen, 73
Walker, Alice, 10, 15
Walker, Lynne, 24
Walker, Rebecca, 15
Washington Post, 56, 128n10
Washington Times, 49–50
Waters, Alice, 46, 65, 128n12
Watt, Jenn, 107
Waxman, Jonathan, 44
Way We Never Were, The (Coontz), 28
#WeAreSHE, 108
Weinstein, Harvey, 101
Weisman, Leslie, 24
Well Fed Network Food Blog Award, 110–11
Weller, Melissa, 133n6
White Papers, Black Marks (Lokko), 131n6
will.i.am, 59
Wilson, Bee, 68
Wilson, Joy, 134n8
'Wichcraft, 128n13

Wizenberg, Molly, 17–18, 64, 72, 107, 110–11, 113–14, 116, 118–20, 129–30n26; awards won, 110–11
"Woman's Place in the Kitchen, A," (Cooper), 99–100, 136n3
"Women and Entrepreneurial Food-Work (Nettles-Barcelón), 64
Women Shaping Shelter, Technology, Consumption, and the Twentieth-Century House (Sharp), 24
women's appetites, 69–71; biblical, 70
Women's E-News, 107
Women's Wear Daily, 133n7
Woolf, Virginia, 11, 85
WordPress, 107
World War II, 23, 28, 37
Wright, Frank Lloyd, 132n16
Wu, Claudia, 65, 134n7
Wu, Elaine, 109

Yabroff, Jennie, 8
Yagoda, Ben, 107
Yahoo Food, 133n7
Yeow, Poh Ling, 71

zine culture, 55

ABOUT THE AUTHOR

Photo credit: Photo by Frank W. Stearns, Jr.

Caroline J. Smith is an associate professor in the University Writing Program at the George Washington University, where she has taught a variety of first-year writing seminars themed around such topics as visual culture, women's writing, and popular culture. She is the author of *Cosmopolitan Culture and Consumerism in Chick Lit* (Routledge, 2007).

CPSIA information can be obtained
at www.ICGtesting.com
Printed in the USA
BVHW071115190423
662607BV00002B/8